How to Build a Business Warren Buffett Would Buy

THE R.C. WILLEY STORY

FOREWORD BY WARREN BUFFETT

Jeff Benedict

SHADOW
MOUNTAIN

DEDICATION

To Tennyson, my twelve-year-old son,
who started his own business last year.

You are a true outlier, logging countless hours after school, at night, and on the weekends to bake homemade desserts and deliver them to customers' homes and offices; to cater events; and to sell your pies, breads, and cookies to stores. Yes, you are sacrificing "play time" for work time. But you love what you do and people love to eat what you create with your hands. I'm so glad you're not like all the other guys. Making things and daring to be different are hallmarks of entrepreneurship. In your early youth you are learning the ropes of success. You never know . . . you may be building the kind of business Warren Buffett would buy. One thing's for sure, you've made your father and mother immensely proud.

Visit us at ShadowMountain.com

Library of Congress Cataloging-in-Publication Data

Benedict, Jeff.
How to build a business Warren Buffett would buy : the R.C. Willey story / Jeff Benedict.
    p.   cm.
Includes index.
ISBN 978-1-60641-041-7 (hardbound : alk. paper)
1. RC Willey Home Furnishings—History. 2. House furnishings industry and trade—United States. 3. Willey, R. C. (Rufus Call), 1900–1954.
4. Child, Bill. I. Title.
HD9773.U7R373 2009
338.7'6450973—dc22   2008050302

Printed in the United States of America
R. R. Donnelley, Crawfordsville, IN

10   9   8   7   6   5   4   3   2   1

CONTENTS

Contents

WARREN BUFFETT

■ ■ ■

FOREWORD

B ill Child represents the best of America. In matters of family, philanthropy, business, or just plain citizenship, anyone who follows in his footsteps is heading true north.

I became Bill's partner in 1995 when Berkshire purchased R.C. Willey. Bill had built that business from sales of $250,000 to a level of $257 million in the year of our purchase. There is nothing easy about the home furnishings business. Bill originally dealt with competitors far larger in sales volume, far better known with consumers, and far better capitalized. But by doing the right things for his customers and associates, he eventually left all of these once-stronger competitors in the dust.

He didn't do this by inventing something new. He just applied the oldest and soundest principle ever set forth:

Treat the other fellow as you would like to be treated yourself. By consistently following this principle he transformed a hole-in-the-wall operation in the tiny town of Syracuse into a business that enjoys the trust of millions of his fellow citizens in Utah.

All along the way, Bill has shared his success with others. Berkshire bought R.C. Willey with its Class A shares, and I've watched Bill quietly dispense those shares in ways to help people less fortunate than he. He lives the principles to which some others apply only lip service.

Just as I have benefited enormously from knowing Bill personally, you can benefit by getting to know him vicariously through this book. Take the lessons from his life and apply them to your own. You will lead a happier, more productive life as a result.

WARREN E. BUFFETT

■ ■ ■

ACKNOWLEDGMENTS

I met Bill Child shortly after I began teaching at Southern Virginia University. At the time, Bill and his wife, Pat, were serving a volunteer mission for The Church of Jesus Christ of Latter-day Saints in Washington, D.C. We became instant friends during our first interview in Kensington, Maryland. People like Bill and Pat remind me just how great the world can be. And forming relationships with people like them is chief among the many privileges of being a writer.

Bill was the perfect gentleman and a relentless stickler for accuracy. More importantly, he's genuinely one of the nicest human beings I've ever met.

Likewise, his brother, Sheldon Child, and the rest of Bill's longtime associates at R.C. Willey were nothing but a pleasure to interview and work with. I'm particularly grateful to Bill's assistant, Sherry Gross.

Without Warren Buffett this book would not have happened. After working on this project it is easy to see why Bill and so many others admire and trust him.

Chris Schoebinger was great to work with, a true pro with an eye for detail and the little things that make a big difference in book publishing. Editor Lisa Mangum and publicist Gail Halladay are part of a great team at Shadow Mountain that moved this project along.

As always, I'm most grateful to my best friend in life, my wife, Lydia. Being in love makes it so much easier to perform as a journalist and a writer. And I'm so grateful for my children, Tennyson Ford, Clancy Nolan, Maggie May, and Clara Belle.

CHAPTER ONE

■ ■ ■

A LETTER FROM WARREN

March 9, 1995
Salt Lake City, Utah

Gripping a Federal Express envelope from Warren Buffett, sixty-three-year-old Bill Child closed his office door at R.C. Willey Home Furnishings' corporate headquarters. The CEO and principal shareholder of Utah's biggest furniture chain wanted to be alone. For months, investment bankers had been trying to entice him to sell his company, dangling more than $200 million in front of him. Numerous national furniture chains had offered a similar price. Bill had turned them all down, convinced he'd only sell to Buffett.

But would Buffett want to buy?

A couple of weeks earlier, the two men had talked by phone about R.C. Willey and the prospect of Berkshire Hathaway Inc.—Buffett's holding company—acquiring it.

On the surface, Buffett liked what he heard. But he had asked to see a little history on the company and the financial statements from the previous two or three years. Buffett had promised to review them and then let Bill know in writing whether he'd be making an offer.

Bill opened the envelope and slowly removed Buffett's letter, marked "personal and confidential." Anxious, he paused. It was hard to believe that he was dealing one-on-one with the man who controlled the conglomerate with the highest-priced shares on the New York Stock Exchange. Buffett had a significant stake in American Express, the Coca-Cola Company, Wells Fargo bank, the Washington Post Company, GEICO, and scores of other highly respected companies and corporations—and now he was actually thinking about buying a company that Bill had spent his life building.

Forty years earlier, at age 22, Bill had taken over his father-in-law's retail appliance store, a 600-square-foot cinder-block building on the edge of a cornfield in remote Syracuse, Utah. At the time, the business was in debt and its only asset was a three-quarter-ton pickup truck used for home deliveries. With no business experience, Bill set out to make the store profitable. A few years later, he convinced his younger brother Sheldon to join him.

Sheldon turned out to be a master salesman and a superb merchant. Bill mastered everything else, from business management to customer service to marketing and advertising. A great team, the brothers spent nearly every day together for thirty-three years, growing their business. In addition to appliances, they started selling furniture and ended up building twelve additions onto their Syracuse store, ultimately making it the single largest appliance and furniture store in Utah. Eventually, additional R.C. Willey stores opened in and around Salt Lake City. By end of 1994, the business was doing more than $250 million per year in sales and controlled more than fifty percent of all furniture sales and more than one-third of all the electronics sold in the state.

Dozens of photographs displayed on Bill's office walls and furniture tops captured a career packed with professional achievement, nonstop growth, and satisfied customers and employees. It had been a great ride. But Bill was getting older and wanted to retire soon. Sheldon was ready for a change, too. They were at a point in their lives when selling the company made some sense.

Yet Bill kept saying no to every offer that came along. Money wasn't the issue; $200 million was an unimaginable sum. Rather, what had kept Bill from saying yes to an offer was his concern for the store's legacy. Over a couple generations, tens of thousands of loyal customers had come to rely on R.C. Willey as a hometown store that always put service ahead of profits and never opened on Sundays. These attributes also had a lot to do with why so many employees stayed with the company for decades. All that would surely change under new ownership.

Bill couldn't accept the idea of turning over control of their family-run operation to bankers or competitors. His brother fully agreed. But holding onto the business wasn't a good option either. It consisted of 1,000 shares of privately held stock, none of which had an assigned value. Bill held the majority of the shares. Sheldon was also a shareholder in the company. And Bill's children each held a limited number of shares. If Bill or Sheldon died, under the federal estate tax regulations the heirs would face a death tax of fifty-five percent of the assessed value of the business, as determined by the IRS. An evaluation of $200 million would require a death tax well over $100 million. Then the remaining shareholders would have no choice but to sell the business, possibly at a fire-sale price.

Bill felt locked in. Finding a buyer willing to maintain status quo on R.C. Willey's management philosophy and one able to address Bill and Sheldon's personal concerns about estate taxes and inheritance seemed like a long shot.

But Buffett had a reputation for acquiring highly successful companies and taking a hands-off approach toward the management team and company philosophy. He also provided a great solution to the death tax by offering to pay for companies with shares of Berkshire Hathaway stock or cash. Since the Berkshire stock was registered with the New York Stock Exchange, Bill and Sheldon would suddenly have an assigned value to their holdings and the transaction would enable their children to acquire shares of Berkshire stock. The inheritance problem would be resolved through an easy distribution.

With so much riding on Buffett's letter, Bill started reading.

"Thanks very much for sending along the audits and

additional information about your company," Buffett wrote. "It is obvious that you have a jewel of an operation. Financial statements frequently give a clue to the personality and character of an enterprise—and the statements of R.C. Willey paint a great portrait."

Bill took a deep breath. The world's greatest investor had just issued his stamp of approval on the company Bill had taken from a one-room store to a dominant home furnishing retail chain.

"I could promise you a transaction," Buffett's letter continued, "that would be 100% certain to close and that would absolutely minimize any distraction to your management and employees."

Those were the magic words. Buffett was promising an ownership change that would go virtually unnoticed by customers and employees. It was the perfect solution.

"I will send you a letter by Federal Express on March 13 that will outline what we would be able to do," Buffett concluded. "Whatever the outcome, you have my admiration for developing a truly outstanding business."

Ecstatic, Bill couldn't wait to tell his brother. No one else would fully appreciate, much less believe, the humble beginnings of the company that Warren Buffett was about to buy.

■ ■ ■

CHAPTER TWO

FROM LINEMAN TO SALESMAN

Summer 1917
Syracuse, Utah

Located west of the Wasatch Mountains and twenty-five miles north of Salt Lake City, Syracuse was a nameless, barren frontier when Mormon pioneers poured into the Utah Territory behind Brigham Young in the mid-1800s. Under the Homestead Act, the first settler arrived in the eight-square-mile region overlooking the eastern shore of the Great Salt Lake and planted the first grain crop there in 1876. A year later, the first log cabin went up. With no local political body in place to select a name for the rapidly forming community, a local salt maker started putting "Syracuse" on his salt bags, borrowing the name from a salt company he knew about back in Syracuse, New York.

The name stuck. First, a businessman built the Syracuse Bathing Resort along the only stretch of the Great Salt

Lake's shoreline that had natural trees. Then the Union Pacific Railroad put down a rail spur in 1877 to connect the resort to the main rail line running between Salt Lake City and Ogden. The new spur was called the Ogden and Syracuse Railway. From then on area residents started calling their new hometown Syracuse.

The Mormon settlers' ingenuity quickly turned the dry desert land into thriving farms. Artesian wells with cement catch basins were constructed, and a canal was built to bring in water from the Weber River. Grain crops fed dairy cattle and paved the way for the creation of a cheese factory, while irrigation from canals in the nearby mountains enabled Syracuse farmers to emerge as some of the leading producers of staple fruits such as apples, pears, peaches, and plums, as well as vegetable row crops, and wheat, barley, and alfalfa.

As farms sprung up, a community emerged: a red brick schoolhouse, a general store, a post office, a canning factory, a mercantile, and a lumberyard. And in 1898 the first Mormon meetinghouse was erected on the main road into town—then known simply as "The Syracuse Road."

Life in Syracuse was simple and comfortably familiar. Virtually everyone went to the same church. Children of all ages attended one school. And everybody made a living off agriculture. Rufus Call Willey—who went by his initials "RC"—grew up this way. But he was destined to be different. Born on January 12, 1900, the seventh of eleven children, he had a fearless willingness to see beyond Syracuse and a natural curiosity about how things worked. RC wanted to do something other than farm. His opportunity came in 1917.

That year he got the chance to work on something that people in Syracuse didn't know much about—electricity. Five years earlier, a new company called Utah Power & Light had formed, not long after Salt Lake City became only the fifth city in the world to have central station electricity. With the power company supplying electricity to roughly 50,000 customers in communities in and around Salt Lake City, it was looking to extend the service to more outlying communities. Syracuse was on the list.

In order to electrify Syracuse, linemen were needed to erect poles and string wire. The work was physically demanding and unquestionably risky. One day it would be backbreaking digging. The next day might entail scaling very high poles. None of that scared off RC. Tall, thin, and strong, the seventeen-year-old boy quit school and jumped at the job.

For the next five years he dug post holes, set utility poles, and then climbed them in order to run wires between them. At twenty-two, he married his seventeen-year-old sweetheart, Helen Swaner, a Salt Lake City resident who he'd met at Lagoon, an amusement park where Swaner sold concessions. By then, Thomas Edison's discovery of the light bulb was forty-four years past, and he had partnered with J.P. Morgan and the Vanderbilt family to form Edison Electric Light Company in New York City. Many homes in the Northeast had electricity, but few of the family farms in

Syracuse were wired. Looking ahead, RC took part-time classes and became a certified electrician.

RC's decision to get in on the ground floor of the effort to light up Syracuse paid off. The power company made him manager of the local substation in Farmington Canyon, which would feed electricity to homes in Syracuse and the rest of Davis County. In his new capacity, RC got acquainted with another big company founded by Edison: General Electric.

As substation manager, RC made trips to Graybar Electric in Salt Lake City to pick up parts and inspect home appliances that required electricity. There were radios, toasters, irons, and other modern conveniences coming out. Hotpoint, a General Electric subsidiary that got its name from the hot tip point on its irons, was rolling out the latest, new home appliance—the refrigerator. RC decided to surprise his wife with one.

It took him a while to save enough money to make the purchase. But everything changed the day he trucked the refrigerator from Salt Lake City and installed it in the home he had built and wired. His wife loved the appliance. So did all her friends. Neighbors kept stopping by just to look at it. RC found himself explaining how it worked and touting the benefits of home refrigeration. Milk and other food products could be kept cold overnight simply by plugging in an appliance. The concept had people talking, especially the wives of farmers.

All of this gave RC an idea: Why not sell refrigerators to his neighbors? He could certainly use the extra income; he had a young, growing family to support. RC approached the electric company and its distributor about becoming a part-time appliance salesman in Syracuse.

The utility company was all for RC's idea. After all, it wanted to sell electricity. Appliances such as refrigerators run 24 hours a day. But that didn't do the utility any good unless the appliances got into people's homes. Graybar Electric— the Hotpoint appliance distributor—supported RC's plan, too, and even offered incentives based on high sales.

RC approached his friend John "Dick" Gailey, the president of Barnes Banking Company in nearby Kaysville. Gailey approved a small line of credit for RC to purchase an initial inventory of a few appliances. And in 1932, RC began selling door-to-door out of the back of his pickup truck. At that time, most of the homes in the area depended on an old-fashioned icebox and utilized a coal-burning stove for cooking and heating. But when RC approached with a refrigerator, frugal farmers consistently told him the same thing: we can't afford one.

RC had a soft response. "I'll tell you what," RC would say. "Just use it for a week. And if you don't want it after a week, I'll come back and take it out—no obligation."

With nothing to lose, farmers took the appliance on a trial basis. RC would wire the home, and the farmer's wife would begin using the refrigerator immediately. Once she experienced what it was like to keep milk and produce cold day and night, she didn't want to revert to life without home refrigeration. When RC returned a week or two later, the homemakers wouldn't let him take back his refrigerators.

Farmers had to figure out how to pay for the appliance.

RC had an answer for that, too—credit. He told his customers they could purchase the appliance on a payment plan, the same way farmers purchased seed grain and other agricultural supplies and equipment. Credit payments were made annually in the fall, when crops were harvested and sold.

It didn't take RC long to realize he could give up his day job altogether and focus exclusively on selling appliances. He made a $15 to $20 profit from selling one refrigerator. That was more than a week's wages working for the power company.

Selling was also a lot more fun. The skills he needed to succeed in sales—an easy ability to talk to people and make them comfortable, superior knowledge about appliances, and enthusiasm for the products—were second nature to him.

RC was also building valuable relationships at the utility company, with the appliance distributor, and at Hotpoint. In 1939, the manufacturer asked RC to help oversee its display at the Golden Gate International Exposition on San Francisco's Treasure Island, an event that coincided with the World's Fair in New York. There he rubbed shoulders with businessmen and entrepreneurs from around the world. He fit right in.

RC brought his wife, Helen, along and together they discovered how much they enjoyed traveling. Now he had an even bigger incentive to sell—Hotpoint promised more complimentary trips to more places based on sales volume.

Summer 1947

Lamar Sessions tried to enlist in the military during World War II. But a few minor medical conditions disqualified him so instead, he ended up working as a transportation specialist at the U.S. Naval base not far from Syracuse. He remained there after the war, learning to drive and maintain virtually every vehicle on the base.

One day Sessions, a short and wiry man, ran into his friend RC Willey. They were fishing buddies. And the two men sometimes took their wives dancing together. Lately, however, RC had been too busy for anything other than work. Appliance sales had practically ground to a halt after the United States entered the war, but now that the war was over, appliance manufacturers were cranking out refrigerators, freezers, Dexter twin tub ringer washing machines, and electric ranges. RC's business had picked up so fast that he couldn't keep up. He needed someone to help make deliveries, do installations, and repair appliances.

"Lamar, why don't you come work for me?" asked RC, promising to keep him employed full-time.

For Sessions it was an easy call. "Ruf" (pronounced "Roof") was his best friend. And delivering and repairing appliances would be a nice change of pace. He told his friend yes.

At age thirty-four, Sessions started working full-time for RC on October 1, 1947. RC gave him his International pickup truck for deliveries, and to drive back and forth to work. The truck wasn't pretty, but it was dependable. On nights when the temperature dropped below zero, Sessions let the truck run all night to ensure he wouldn't have trouble starting it the next morning.

It was all Sessions could do to keep up with RC, who was selling appliances faster than they could be delivered. Every time Hotpoint rolled out a new appliance, RC had Syracuse customers buying it. When Sylvania started making televisions, RC had to hire a couple of more guys to work part-time helping Sessions with installations.

Since RC did all his business door-to-door, he didn't have a store. He simply kept his inventory in a two-car garage behind his house. But his competitors eventually complained to the distributor, arguing that the absence of any overhead gave RC an unfair advantage when it came to pricing. They insisted that RC be required to either have a retail store or lose his franchise with the distributor.

Technically, RC Willey's competitors had a fair point—Hotpoint was supposed to deal exclusively with stores, not just anyone selling appliances out of his home or garage. But since RC was the top salesman in the area, Hotpoint didn't want to lose his business. Sales representative Alan Searel recommended that RC erect a simple store to quiet his competitors.

In 1949, RC built a 600-square-foot, cinderblock building with a white stucco exterior right next door to his home. He ran the electricity from the house to the store, along with a telephone line that tied into the house. The store had no indoor plumbing. But it had three large showroom windows with appliances behind them. Outside it had a gravel parking area for four cars and a neon sign mounted to the front of the building—Hotpoint Appliances: R.C. WILLEY. He was now a legitimate appliance dealer in full compliance with the distributor's policies.

Aside from the cost of the construction, the store did nothing to raise his overhead costs or raise his rock-bottom prices. His property was off an old farm road, far enough from the town center that it attracted no foot traffic. Most of his business continued to be generated by word of mouth and over the telephone. So RC rigged up a nine-party telephone line, with an outdoor bell system that enabled him to hear incoming calls if he was working in his backyard or loading appliances onto the truck.

The building gave RC a home base of operation and a place to showcase his appliances. It was also where Sessions reported each morning to get his delivery assignments for the day. One day Sessions met RC at the store after making some morning deliveries in Syracuse.

"Lamar, take this television down to the west part of West Point," he said. "It goes to the home right next to Reese Montgomery's place."

Sessions lived in West Point and knew the area well enough. He put the television on the truck and drove along a dirt road that ran right down to the Great Salt Lake. At that time none of the homes had street addresses. He went to the house next door to Reese Montgomery.

No one was home.

As was customary when encountering customers who weren't at home, Sessions entered and installed the television. Then he went up on the roof and mounted an antenna, referred to as an aerial.

The next morning when Sessions reported to work, RC was waiting for him out front, dressed in wool trousers, a heavy flannel shirt, and a Stetson hat—his typical outfit.

"Hey, where'd you put that television?" RC asked.

"Right where you told me, Ruf," Sessions said.

"No, you didn't."

A man had called RC at the store and informed him that he had gotten home and discovered a television inside. Sessions had mistakenly entered the home next door to the intended customer's residence and installed the television and antenna.

"But we sold it anyway," RC said, explaining he had talked the man into keeping the television.

Sessions was relieved.

"Now," RC told him, "go put this one up in the right place."

Both men laughed.

Sessions marveled at RC's ability to convince people to buy things, even when they weren't looking to make a purchase. Every time the two men went hunting or fishing out of state, RC never failed to sell an appliance to someone they encountered in the woods.

Sometimes RC turned sporting trips into blockbuster sales outings. Shortly after RC built his store, he and Sessions went fishing for a week in Yellowstone. During the entire time, Sessions didn't see RC talk with anyone about appliances. But when they returned to Syracuse, RC surprised Sessions with some instructions.

"Lamar," he said, "load these electric ranges on the trailer and take them up to Yellowstone."

He was pointing to a line of apartment-size, electric ranges. Unbeknownst to Sessions, RC had convinced the owner of the campsite where they had stayed to buy a range for every cabin at the campsite. Campers would surely pay more for a cabin equipped with a stove that allowed guests the luxury of cooking with the turn of a dial. The offer to deliver and install the appliances overcame any other hesitations on the part of the camp owner.

"RC once told me," Sessions recalled, "the basis of being a good salesman is always having an answer ready for anything they might come up with. If a potential customer has a qualm or dislike, you have to have an answer. And he did. He always had an answer."

The more RC sold, the more vacations he and his wife took at Hotpoint's expense. He even sold when he was supposed to be taking time off. Once, while flying back from a complimentary vacation with his wife, he pitched a washing machine to the airline stewardess. She liked what she heard but politely declined, saying it was impossible for her to buy from RC. After all, she lived thousands of miles away in Hawaii.

That didn't deter RC. He closed the sale at 30,000 feet when he offered to ship the appliance from his store in Utah to the stewardess's home in Hawaii. He had no idea what it would cost to ship a washer that far. The overseas freight charges ended up exceeding the sale price he had quoted the stewardess.

Knowing he'd take a loss on the transaction, RC nonetheless kept his word. He judged success on satisfied customers and sales volume, not profit margins. That's what kept people coming back to him for purchases, time and time again.

Another reason RC was so good at selling is that everyone he met was a potential customer. Even when dining out with the family at a nice restaurant, he had a habit of pitching appliances to waitresses. It always made his wife uncomfortable.

"Now, RC," Helen told him one night after they sat down at an upscale restaurant, "don't you embarrass me by trying to sell to these waitresses. Let's just have a nice dinner and not worry about trying to sell anything."

"Well, dear," he said, "you know we like these nice dinners and the only way we can afford them is if I keep selling."

That evening, after the meal, he asked the waitress to bring out the cook so he could compliment him. When the cook appeared at the table, RC praised his culinary skills.

The cook appreciated the compliment.

"Now look," RC told him, "do you need a new refrigerator or an electric range?"

The cook was caught off guard. Helen was perplexed.

"I can save you a lot of money," RC continued. "I've got a little store out in Syracuse."

When the prospect of a sale was on his mind, he easily lost sight of everything else, including the time and place.

This was especially true if he thought he might lose a sale. One Sunday he cornered Sessions in the foyer at church.

"Lamar," RC said hurriedly, "you ought to go down to Hooper and take care of Howard Widdison."

A few days earlier RC had talked Widdison into buying an appliance. But he hadn't closed the deal. He wanted Sessions to go see him later that afternoon.

"Ruf, you know what day it is," Sessions said discreetly.

"I know," RC said. "But we'll lose him if we don't. We'll lose him."

Sessions had to smile at his friend. One reason he admired RC so much was that there was nothing pretentious about him. Irresistibly honest, RC was the kind of guy you wanted to work for and to buy from—he was a natural-born salesman.

If he could have figured out a way to sell in his sleep, RC would have done it. But Sessions didn't want to approach a customer on Sunday.

The more RC thought about it, the more he agreed. In those days, businesses in Utah were not open on Sunday, and the notion of treating Sunday as a day of rest was widely accepted. RC had just gotten a little excited. He thought better of the idea and insisted the Widdison sale could wait until first thing Monday morning.

RC's everyone's-a-customer philosophy paid off. At the end of 1950, his business had achieved its most successful year yet, reaching $50,000 in annual sales. He did it all with just one full-time employee. It's what led people who knew him to consider him the best salesman in all of Utah.

CHAPTER THREE

■ ■ ■

THE KEYS TO THE STORE

Business wasn't the only thing growing for RC Willey. His family was branching out too. In 1951, his youngest daughter, Helen Darline Willey, married nineteen-year-old Bill Child, her high school boyfriend. RC was especially fond of his youngest daughter, who had been named after her mother, yet went by her middle name. Darline's choice for a husband pleased RC.

Like RC, Child wanted a career in something other than agriculture. Born and raised on a nearby Syracuse farm, Child had determined the occupation was just too unpredictable. Feed costs, produce prices, and weather were all factors outside an individual farmer's control. Yet these things had a direct impact on a farmer's income, making it very difficult to predict earnings from one year to the next.

Child hoped to avoid the financial uncertainties his father had experienced while laboring away on the family farm.

Besides, he wanted a job where he could use his mind more. Child settled on becoming a teacher. He entered the Naval Reserve Officer Training program right out of high school and enrolled in classes at Weber State College. He completed his first year of college just weeks before marrying Darline. A couple of months later, he transferred to the University of Utah, after the school offered him a scholarship.

To be closer to campus, Bill and Darline rented a small apartment in Salt Lake City. It was the first time either of them had lived outside Syracuse. RC and his wife hated to see their daughter move away, but they appreciated Bill's dedication to achieving his education and professional goals.

At the end of Bill's second year of college, Darline was expecting their first child. Eager to get their daughter back in Syracuse, RC and his wife gave Darline and Bill a small lot on their property. The couple gladly gave up their apartment and purchased a prefabricated house for $5,200. RC's friend Dick Gailey gave the Childs a mortgage of just over $4,000 to help with the purchase. Bill sold some cattle he'd been raising on his dad's farm for the down payment. Plus, RC helped provide appliances and asked his nephew Jay Willey to wire the place. Bill put the house fifty yards from RC Willey's store and moved back home.

By the time Bill and Darline had their first child in 1952, Bill had two years of college remaining. That summer he started working full-time for RC. Strong, athletic, and accustomed to tough physical labor, Child had no trouble handling the heavy lifting and other physical aspects of the appliance store. Some days he'd help Lamar Sessions make deliveries and installations. Other days he'd unload inventory or work alongside RC, making sales and interacting with customers.

RC appreciated Child's work ethic. But what really impressed him was his son-in-law's natural way with people. Handsome and unusually well-mannered, Child had a way of putting people at ease. And without being prompted, he instinctively went out of his way to attend to customers' needs and questions when they entered the store.

Before long, RC asked Bill to start working nights with him. Early evening is when most customers visited the store. Bill would demonstrate how the appliances worked and answer questions about specific features while RC negotiated the purchase price and put together the paperwork on the transaction.

The arrangement worked well. With Bill in the store alongside RC, Darline spent many evenings next door with her mother, who helped out with the baby. The business had a way of keeping the family close to home. The more Child worked with his father-in-law, the fonder the two became of each other. Every Saturday they'd close the store to attend the local baseball game. Leaving the store unlocked, they'd simply hang a sign on the door: "Gone to the ballgame . . . Come in and look around."

When Bill returned to school for his final year of classes

in the fall of 1953, he continued working nights and Saturdays in the store.

Lamar Sessions was relieved that RC had hired an extra set of hands. It was all he could do to keep up with deliveries and service calls. A lot of the brand-new appliances had a tendency to have mechanical glitches that required maintenance and repairs. Determined to keep his customers happy, RC had Sessions making house calls every time someone complained of a problem. This was on top of the increasingly heavy delivery schedule for installing new appliances.

Sessions didn't mind, though. RC always paid him generously. And despite how busy things had gotten, the two men still made time for regular hunting and fishing expeditions, along with evenings out with their wives.

But in the spring of 1954, RC started feeling discomfort in his stomach and his appetite tailed off. He figured he had ulcers brought on by stress. The business was having a record-breaking year and was on track to hit $250,000 in sales—a remarkable volume for any appliance store at that time, but especially for one that only had two full-time employees and one part-time college kid working nights and weekends. The burden to keep it all together fell squarely on RC.

He tried working through the pain, but it kept increasing. Worse, it spread to other parts of his body. One afternoon he pulled Sessions aside and told him he needed a vacation and was going to California for a couple weeks with his wife. He told his friend to keep the business going until he returned.

Unaware of just how poorly RC felt, Sessions protested. He was booked solid with deliveries and repairs. And with Hotpoint rolling out a new line of washing machines, customers were clamoring for the new model. There was no way, Sessions argued, he'd be able to manage in-store sales and purchases on top of his other duties. Besides, if RC left for California he'd risk losing a bunch of sales.

RC didn't disagree. Nonetheless, without elaborating on his physical condition, RC said he was going despite how busy things were at the store.

Sessions didn't get it. RC's behavior was so out of character.

"You know, Lamar," RC finally said, "when you think you're going to die, you'll do most anything to prolong your life."

A Couple of Days Later

The date was marked on Bill's calendar: June 1, 1954. Graduation day had finally arrived. That morning Bill received his diploma from the University of Utah. Better still, he had already lined up a job. The principal of the junior high school in Syracuse had offered him a contract to start teaching in the fall for an annual salary of almost $2,500, plus summers off. All Bill had to do was sign.

There was a lot to celebrate. Bill and Darline were about to start a new chapter in their life. RC could not have been happier for his son-in-law. Hours after the commencement ceremony concluded, he visited Bill at his house. While there, RC explained that he and his wife were heading to California for some time off.

"I need to rest and get rid of these ulcers," RC told Bill.

Bill hadn't realized his father-in-law had been feeling poorly. He agreed that a vacation sounded like a good idea.

RC said he had a favor to ask. He wanted Bill to oversee the store while he was away.

Bill offered to do whatever his father-in-law needed.

RC handed him the keys to the store. "Take care of it," RC said. "I'll be back in two weeks."

The minute RC left, Bill realized there was a lot more to running an appliance business than selling refrigerators and washing machines. Customers had all kinds of questions from service and maintenance to delivery schedules. Every time Bill turned around, it seemed, someone was on the phone in need of something urgent.

Selling had other elements, too. Whenever an appliance went out the door, records had to be kept and funds had to be properly recorded and deposited. Bill and Lamar were scrambling. RC had only been gone a few days, and Bill couldn't wait for him to return.

Suddenly, Bill saw RC's vehicle pass the storefront and park in the driveway. RC and his wife weren't supposed to be home for another week. Confused, Bill ran next door.

His mother-in-law explained that RC was feeling too ill to vacation. Without saying much, RC went into the house and directly to bed, where he stayed for the next two days. Unsure what was the matter, the family took him to the hospital. It didn't take doctors long to diagnose the source of the problem: pancreatic cancer.

The family couldn't believe it. RC was just 54 years old and only weeks earlier he looked full of life. Overnight, everything had changed. Uncertainty surrounded RC's future. Doctors weren't sure he'd even be able to return home.

Now Bill's future was up in the air, too. He had a teaching contract offer to sign. But there wasn't anyone else who could run the business, which supported virtually everyone in the family. Plus, there were financial obligations to distributors and vendors, the bank, and countless customers. This was no longer the simple door-to-door sales business that RC had started more than twenty years earlier. R.C. Willey Appliances was a thriving small company with a glowing reputation.

Bill felt as though he had no choice but to forego the teaching contract. But even if he did, would the business survive without RC? After all, to his customers, RC Willey *was* the company.

There was a lot to sort out.

Shortly after RC entered the hospital, Bill took a call at the store. The man introduced himself as Vern Burton, an IRS agent who had been assigned to conduct an audit of the R.C. Willey store.

Bill wasn't entirely sure what an IRS agent was. It had only been a year since the U.S. Treasury officially created the name "Internal Revenue Agency" for the federal government's tax collection bureau. But Bill certainly knew the

terms *audit* and *government* and that the call probably sig-
naled trouble. He asked if something was wrong.

Burton said the company hadn't made any tax payments
to the federal government. He wanted to set up a time to
come in and examine the company's books.

There must be some kind of mix-up, Bill figured. The
taxes—along with all the other bills—were paid by RC
Willey's outside accountant. RC was not a numbers guy.
That's why he had hired someone to handle the bookkeeping. Bill called the accountant and demanded answers.

The accountant didn't bother explaining. Instead, he
showed up at the Willey's house when no one was around
and dropped off the checkbook, the check register, and all
financial records and invoices on the front step.

Taxes, it turned out, weren't the only thing that hadn't
been paid. Bill discovered months' worth of overdue invoices. On one of his nightly trips to the hospital to check
on his father-in-law, Bill had RC sign paperwork authoriz-
ing him to endorse checks from the business account. Then
he immediately started sending payments to accounts that
were past due.

About a week later, he received an abrupt call from Alan
Blood, the vice president and cashier at Barnes Banking
Company, where the R.C. Willey business did its banking.
A very respected and conservative banker, Blood was in line
to succeed Gailey as president; Blood told Bill to stop writ-
ing checks at once.

"You can't write checks when you don't have funds to
cover them," he said.

"But I have been making deposits every day," Bill insisted.

Blood explained that the store's account was deep in the red and the recently deposited funds weren't enough to overcome the negative balance.

"You don't have any money in the bank," Blood repeated.

Bill knew the business account was in the red; he had looked at the previous two bank statements and noted the consistent negative balance. But he also knew that his father-in-law always dealt directly with Dick Gailey, the bank's president. "I assumed," he told Blood, "that the bank had arrangements to cover these checks on some kind of a loan."

"That was between Dick Gailey and RC," Blood said. "But that's got nothing to do with Bill Child."

The message was clear—those days were over.

■ ■ ■

CHAPTER FOUR

JUST HANG ON

No one expected the end to come so fast. RC slipped quietly into a coma and died on September 3, 1954. He never left the hospital after being admitted on the heels of his shortened trip to California at the start of the summer.

RC's wife, Helen, couldn't get used to life without him. While he had been hospitalized, she spent a lot of time next door at Bill and Darline's home, especially in the evenings. Now she needed them more than ever.

The loss took a toll on Bill, too. RC was like a second father to him, a larger-than-life figure who had a contagious enthusiasm for work, family, and leisure. At twenty-two, Bill had never experienced the loss of someone so close. Without RC around, the store felt empty and cold.

Other factors were sapping Bill's zeal for the business. The IRS had begun its audit. The bank had clamped down on the store's tendency to sell on credit. And customers regularly made service requests on electric appliances. Dealing with all this had very little appeal for Bill.

Normally, Dick Gailey handled any problems that surfaced involving the R.C. Willey credit and banking account by talking directly with RC. But Gailey was on an extended vacation in Europe, and the store's credit crisis needed immediate attention. Alan Blood waited until the funeral proceedings were concluded before he invited Bill to come in and see him at the bank. He suggested that RC's wife come, too.

When Bill entered the bank cashier's office with his mother-in-law, he wasn't sure what to expect. Blood wanted to make sure the family knew just what kind of financial shape the business was in. He painted a grim picture.

Two years earlier RC had borrowed $9,000 from the bank to build his warehouse after a fire destroyed his double-car garage and all the appliances he had been storing there. But he had never made a single payment on the loan. There were interest payments due on top of the principal.

There was a bigger problem stemming from RC's credit arrangements with his customers. The deal was simple. RC would sell an appliance for $100. The customer would put down $10 cash and finance the rest through the bank. RC would sign a $90 note and send it to the bank, which, in turn, posted a $90 credit to RC's account and sent out a payment notice to the customer. When the due date arrived, most customers paid. But some didn't.

Bill knew there were a few delinquent accounts, and since all contracts were full recourse, meaning that if the customer didn't pay, the bank had the right to hold the store accountable, he was afraid to find out just how many accounts had not paid.

Blood said that the store had about $150,000 worth of credit accounts. Roughly one-third of those customers were current in their payments to the bank; the other two-thirds were behind. Some customers were way behind. Almost one-third of RC's credit customers hadn't made a payment in more than nine months.

The bank had done little to follow up with the delinquent accounts. Neither had RC. He was too busy selling. And as long as sales remained strong, Gailey continued to allow RC's customers to purchase on credit.

But Blood had a different approach. According to the terms of RC's bank contracts, the store had to repurchase roughly $50,000 in delinquent contracts that were eligible for full collection. Blood expected Bill to pay those contracts off at once.

Bill felt as though he had been kicked in the stomach. The decision as to what to do with the business couldn't be put off any longer.

From the bank's perspective, the choice was simple. There was little wisdom in turning over a deeply indebted company to an inexperienced college graduate with aspirations of going into education. Blood looked across the desk at RC's wife. "Helen," he said, "you need to sell the business and let Bill go teach school."

Helen didn't know what to say.

Bill said he and his mother-in-law would discuss it and get back to the bank with an answer.

Bill left the bank frustrated. He had never set out to run a retail business in the first place. He only agreed to take over the store on an interim basis to help out RC, knowing full well that he lacked any formal business training. But the more he thought about the banker's advice, the more he disagreed with it. Selling a business that was deeply in debt didn't make any sense.

There was another problem. Despite all the money RC had made over his career, he hadn't saved any of it. He traveled often, spent lavishly on his wife and family, and gave away a great deal of money anonymously to needy people and causes. Now widowed, his wife had nothing to live off. No one in the family had the means to support her either. Her welfare was entirely in Bill's hands.

Bill knew what he had to do. On a teacher's salary he'd never be able to support his mother-in-law on top of his own family. He talked to Joseph Cook, the principal at the school that had offered him a job.

Cook knew the Willey family, and he was familiar with the situation Bill was facing. He also knew how badly Bill wanted to teach.

"There's no one to run this business," Bill explained. "I'm the only one. So consequently I can't sign that teaching contract."

"You have to run the business," Cook said. "I know that."

Bill admired Cook and still held out hope of one day working for him.

"If you have a teaching position open in the future, would you please consider me?"

"Bill, I would love to have you teach for me," Cook said. "However, my intuition tells me that if you get into business, you'll never teach."

Committed to getting the store on a more solid financial footing, Bill talked his mother-in-law into holding onto the business, at least for the time being. The store, he insisted, really wasn't much of a store. It had no plumbing. The only electrical service was tied to the house, as was the phone service. And the building was located far off the beaten path, next door to a corn patch. On top of all that, the business was in the red. "The problem," he told his mother-in-law, "is that if we sell the business now we have nothing to gain from it."

Bill had seen his own father repeatedly fall on hard financial times in his farming and cattle business by buying and selling at the wrong time. He wasn't going to repeat that mistake. Yes, RC Willey's business was in debt. But on the flip side, the company had a loyal customer base and a stellar reputation. With some financial discipline and sustained hard work, Bill was convinced the company could turn a profit.

"If we can just hang on, we will be okay," Bill told Helen.

CHAPTER FIVE

■ ■ ■

RELATIONSHIPS MATTER

G ive me some time," Bill told Barnes Banking executive
 Alan Blood when he called to confirm that he and his
mother-in-law had decided against closing down the
business.

Blood wasn't enthused. But Bill made a compelling case.
"If we close the business," he said, "there will be no funds to
pay you. If we remain open, we will be able to pay everything off. We have a good business. We just need time."

Recognizing there were inadequate assets to cover the
bank's loans, Blood reluctantly went along.

General Manager. Bill figured that the title suited him.
For a salary, he decided to pay himself $100 per week—the
exact wage that RC had been paying Lamar Sessions for delivering and installing appliances. On weeks when the store

didn't pull in enough money, Bill simply withheld some or all of his own salary.

Long-term, Bill knew he'd have to sell a lot of appliances and televisions—many more than RC had ever sold—to get the business out of the red. But short-term, he needed cash to keep the business afloat. A loan was the obvious solution.

He didn't bother approaching Barnes Banking; he already owed them $9,000 on the warehouse loan, and they were forcing him to buy back all the delinquent appliance loans. Instead, Bill approached the Bank of Utah, where he had recently transferred the store's checking account. RC's wife knew the bank's vice president, who agreed to meet with Bill and review the store's financial needs and its credit worthiness. It seemed like Bill had finally caught a break.

But after thoroughly looking into the appliance store's debts and assets, the Bank of Utah turned down Bill's request for a loan, based on insufficient collateral. The store had no hard assets. The inventory was purchased on credit. There was no cash in the bank. Even the store's showroom and warehouse couldn't be counted; they were built as an attachment to RC's home without a separate deed or title. The bank's vice president told Bill that essentially the only thing the company truly owned was the used pickup truck that RC had used for making deliveries.

Bill shook his head in amazement. RC had made about $250,000 in sales the year prior to his death, yet he had nothing to show for it. He often sold appliances at such low prices that he left himself little to no profit margins. That's one reason his customers were so loyal. Even still, some of the store's credit customers didn't pay their bills.

The bank's rejection taught Bill his first lesson in business—relationships matter. And Bill didn't have any. The fact that RC had a tight relationship with influential businessmen such as the president of Barnes Banking Company didn't mean much after RC died. If Bill was going to keep the business afloat, he had to establish his own connections.

This realization had another important principle behind it—integrity is the foundation of any good relationship. This is especially true in business, where trust is the key to opening doors, extending credit, and cultivating loyal customers.

But earning people's trust takes time and a consistent performance.

Determined to get started, Bill approached the First National Bank of Layton, an institution that competed more directly with Barnes Banking. He explained his predicament to a young banker named George Wilcox, and he made a convincing case for why the bank should loan him $10,000.

Wilcox knew the reputation of RC Willey. More important, he liked what he saw in Bill. By the time the two men satisfied each other's questions, Wilcox said that he thought the bank could meet Bill's needs with a line of credit. "But," Wilcox told him, "I don't normally make loans to people or companies that don't have an account here at the bank."

Bill didn't hesitate. "The account will be here tomorrow," he pledged.

"We're going to get along just great," Wilcox said, extending his hand.

Later that day, Bill closed out the business checking account at the Bank of Utah and transferred it to First National of Layton. Bill's business relationship with a banker had begun.

Before IRS agent Vern Burton completed his audit of R.C. Willey, he concluded the company owed well over $10,000 in past due taxes. That didn't include the interest payments and a substantial penalty for failing to make payments.

Bill didn't dispute the amount owed, nor did he make excuses. However, he explained that he didn't feel qualified to respond to the audit. He didn't have an accounting background and the tax code was new to him. "RC was honest and always met his obligations," Bill told Burton. "He was a man of the highest integrity. But he left all the bookkeeping and tax obligations to his accountant. And when I questioned the accountant about the unpaid bills and this tax audit, he quit."

Burton recognized that Bill had inherited the tax problem, not created it. He also appreciated Bill's candor and his desire to meet the company's obligations to the government.

Talking through the situation, Burton mentioned that one day he hoped to work in the private sector helping small business owners manage their tax obligations. With the IRS being so new, many farmers and small businesses didn't employ accountants and often missed tax deadlines.

The conversation gave Bill an idea. He needed to convince the IRS to be lenient with R.C. Willey. But Bill didn't have time to take on that chore, nor did he know where to begin. Burton, on the other hand, knew the IRS regulations like the back of his hand. He also had a good understanding of R.C. Willey's financial situation. He'd make the ideal accountant for the company.

"I need someone like you to help me," Bill said. "Why don't you come and do our books?"

Burton liked the idea. "You know, I've been thinking about getting into public accounting. If I could get the IRS's approval, would you let me do your bookkeeping and accounting?"

"Yes, obviously," Bill said. "I'd love to have you do our accounting."

After receiving clearance to represent the store against the agency, Burton resigned as an IRS agent and Bill hired him. Another IRS agent was assigned to the case, and Burton successfully defended R.C. Willey's interests, convincing the IRS to reduce all past taxes, interest, and penalties to $10,000.

Rarely do the accused think to hire the accuser. But Bill realized that in order for his store to survive the government's inquiry, he needed to think outside the box. Burton ended up saving the business thousands of dollars, and he cleared the way for the store to remain open. At Bill's request, he stayed on part-time to set up bookkeeping procedures and to handle the company's accounting. Bill found it refreshing to have such a competent, honest accountant. From that day forward, the business never missed a tax payment or a billing deadline, thanks to Vern Burton.

Even though he had closed out his business account at Barnes Banking Company, Bill still had to deal with the bank about the warehouse loan and the delinquent credit customers. Bill had been meeting his obligations, but the debts were gnawing at him. He decided to try a two-pronged approach to settle his debts.

To pay down the $9,000 building loan, he took advantage of an incentive program being offered by the power company. In an attempt to promote electricity, Utah Power & Light promised appliance retailers $35 every time they convinced a customer to replace a gas-fired water heater with an electric one. Similarly, the company offered retailers $25 each time they sold an electric range to replace a gas stove. To collect the incentive payments, the retailer had to turn in the old appliance along with a sales receipt confirming that a new electric appliance had been purchased.

On the sales and marketing side, Bill put all his energy into promoting the advantages of electric water heaters and ranges. At the outset, $9,000 seemed like a big mountain to overcome in $35 and $25 increments. But Bill figured if he sold 150 water heaters and 150 ranges he'd earn $9,000 in incentive payments from the electric company. He started chipping away.

One by one, loyal R.C. Willey customers made the switch. Without exception, Bill applied the bonus payments from Utah Power & Light to the mortgage debt for the warehouse. A little at a time, the loan balance shrunk.

But getting out from under the delinquent credit accounts required a different approach. After some research, Bill discovered a company called Commercial Credit, which loaned money to consumers who might not qualify for traditional lending through a bank. Bill met with Commercial Credit's loan officer Jack Penrod and showed him the delinquent contracts that Barnes Banking had charged back to R.C. Willey.

Penrod agreed to purchase most of the delinquent contracts—known as commercial paper—from Bill. Commercial Credit would then refinance the loans at a higher interest rate. The job of convincing delinquent customers to sign a new credit agreement fell to Bill. He provided them the new contract from Commercial Credit and a simple choice: "You either have to sign the agreement or I have to take back the appliance."

Most of the customers refinanced and the burden of collecting payments instantly shifted from Bill to Commercial Credit. In cases where customers wouldn't refinance, Bill assumed the role of the repossession man. He didn't particularly like the process, but it had to be done to get the company's financial house in order, and there wasn't anyone else around to do it.

Word of his efforts to recover appliances from delinquent customers spread. One Saturday morning the owner of the local gas station called Bill at the store. The station owner reported that a man, who was well-known around town for having outstanding debts, was leaving town and had packed all of his family's possessions onto a moving truck, including a Hotpoint freezer that probably had not been paid for. The truck had overheated and was sitting at the fueling station.

Bill confirmed that R.C. Willey had in fact sold the freezer in question and it had not been paid for.

The station owner told Bill that he was just finishing up with the engine repair. "If you get here quickly, I will hold him," he told Bill.

"I'll be right there," Bill said.

He jumped in his pickup truck and hustled over to the gas station, pulling up just as the family was about to drive away. "I bet you are on your way to deliver that freezer back to us," Bill said with a smile.

"Why, yes," the customer said sheepishly.

"Well, let me help you," Bill said.

After they transferred the freezer onto the R.C. Willey delivery truck, Bill thanked the customer and wished him and his family well.

Despite the confrontational nature of the repossession business, Bill managed to do it with dignity. Occasionally, he needed a little humor, too.

Once, while working down his list of past due customers, Bill went to an address in search of a television. The owners hadn't made a payment in nearly a year. A man answered the door and Bill informed him he was there to retrieve a television due to the man's failure to make payments.

The man let Bill enter and apologized repeatedly for not making his payment. Bill nonetheless disconnected the set and took it to his truck. The customer's wife and children trailed Bill, apologizing and pleading with him not to take the family's TV.

The husband kept insisting that he was only one month behind in his payment. That didn't make sense to Bill and caused a red flag to go up. Once he got the television outside, Bill inspected it more closely. Then it dawned on him—the brand wasn't one that R.C. Willey carried. He checked his records against the address of the residence. The house number matched the paperwork—but Bill was on the wrong street. He should have been on the next block.

Bill felt terrible and hesitated.

"Maybe you can tell me a little more about the circumstances pertaining to this television," Bill said to the father.

The man promised he was going to make his payment immediately. His wife and children huddled around him, looking up at Bill on the back of the truck.

"You know what I'm going to do?" Bill told the father. "I'm going to take this right back in your house because I know you're an honest man and you'll pay your bill."

The children were thrilled and the husband and wife thanked Bill profusely.

He wheeled the television back into the family's house and reinstalled it for them. Then he drove to the correct address on the next street, only to discover that the people had moved.

Bill's hard work continued to pay off. One evening

eighteen-year-old Connie O'Brien entered the store, stating she was looking for a part-time job. Bill wasn't sure what to say. He had known Connie since she was a child, but other than employing Lamar Sessions for deliveries and repairs, the store didn't have employees. Bill did everything himself. RC had always run the store that way, and Bill had no plans to change the way things were done.

"Why don't you wait here a few minutes," Bill suggested. A couple of customers needed his immediate attention on the sales floor.

Connie sat patiently inside a small, one-desk office as Bill hustled between customers. Before long, another customer came through the door. Then the phone started ringing.

Observing that Bill couldn't talk to customers and answer the phone at the same time, Connie picked up.

"R.C. Willey, may I help you?"

Bill was floored. She was so proactive and naturally professional.

The phone rang a few more times before Bill finished up with the customers, and each time Connie answered and took a message. Before long, she was at Bill's desk taking down notes. Bill never had to leave the customers unattended.

This isn't a bad idea, he thought to himself.

Although Connie had no formal business training, she had a charismatic personality. Bill hired her part-time to answer phones and file sales contracts during the late afternoon and early evenings. It left him more time to focus on sales.

It wasn't long before Connie was writing up sales contracts for customers and handling all sorts of clerical responsibilities. Bill realized that if he was going to grow the business, he'd have to rethink RC's business model. By hiring other people, Bill figured, he could increase sales revenue.

Between refinancing and repossessing, Bill managed to eliminate all $50,000 in delinquent contracts held by the Barnes Banking Company. It required him to get his hands dirty and work a lot of twelve-hour days, but in the process, he formed another valuable relationship. He decided to do more business with Jack Penrod and Commercial Credit.

For more than twenty years of selling appliances, RC had always done financing exclusively through his friend Dick Gailey. If a customer couldn't afford to pay cash for an appliance, RC had them sign a credit contract, which he forwarded to the bank. Credit background checks were never performed on customers. Such precautions were not necessary; people generally honored their obligations.

But in the early 1950s, more people began buying on credit. Some of them were overextended and delinquencies rose, which was one of the reasons for the company's credit problems. Drawing off his relationship with Penrod, Bill instituted a new policy for R.C. Willey. Customers seeking to buy appliances on credit were required to complete a credit application. Bill would call it in to Penrod, who checked the applicant's credit worthiness. If Penrod concluded that the customer was a low risk for default, Bill would complete the sale. Otherwise, Bill would work something out with the customer or cancel the delivery altogether.

The business relationship was a success. Penrod acquired lots of new customers and Bill avoided the risk of selling to people who were unlikely to make payments.

■ ■ ■

CHAPTER SIX

Mr. Frugality

May 19, 1955

Even though he was constantly hustling to establish the store's financial footing, Bill had no worries about his personal finances. Only a few years after buying their first home, he and Darline had completely paid off the mortgage.

As the president of the bank holding the mortgage, Dick Gailey personally wrote Bill a letter to congratulate him.

"Dear Billy," he began. "Your check to cover the balance of your loan came this morning and you will find enclosed a cancelled note, Title Policy, and a release of mortgage and deed. Your father-in-law at one time told me that you are sure to become a wealthy man.

"Ask yourself one question: Can I save money? If the answer is no, it is better to get a job and work for the other fellow. The only man that can handle a business and do well is one that can save money. I am sure that you can give YES as the answer."

Bill admired Gailey, and he treasured the letter. Although quite a bit younger, Bill shared Gailey's philosophy toward money long before he started running his own business. While attending the University of Utah, Bill used to get his hair cut by a man who put a sign along the main highway to Salt Lake City, advertising haircuts for 65 cents. His scissors were a little crude and the hair cream he applied afterward left a lot to be desired. But Bill went to him because the guy was cheaper than all the barbers in Syracuse or Salt Lake City.

Bill's spending habits didn't change when he took over the store. Instead of buying a new car, he drove an old one. He rarely spent money on himself. His biggest problem was that he worked all the time; if the store was open, he was there. His schedule left no time for discretionary spending. His big excursion was taking the family to Clearfield for hamburgers and malts at Hawkins Drive-in.

His wife, Darline, was just as frugal. Bill would give her money and say, "Go buy yourself a new dress." Instead, she'd come back with something for the children. She had everything she needed and simply didn't have any desire for luxuries. This commitment to modest living is what enabled them to be mortgage-free after only a few years.

Bill was just as frugal with the company's resources. He kept his salary at a modest level. When it came to bonuses, he always reinvested them in the business, never drawing them for lavish living. He maintained this lean lifestyle even after the company started turning a profit. And he was very reluctant to spend company money unless the expense bore a direct relationship to creating a sale or expanding growth and development.

Around the time that Bill took over the R.C. Willey store, Hotpoint introduced a new automatic washing machine featuring a clutch-operated centrifuge that spun clothing fast and evenly. The supposedly innovative technology promised to be a major step-up from the previously reliable fluid drive models.

Bill didn't waste any time. Everyone who came into the store looking for a washing machine was introduced to this automatic model. Compared to the conventional ringer washers, it was like going from a horse and buggy to an automobile. Housewives realized they could save a lot of time and energy with a machine that handled all the washing, rinsing, and partial drying by itself.

The machines sold for approximately $219, an excellent value for those days. Between 1954 and 1955, Bill sold 400 of Hotpoint's new automatic machines, single-handedly outselling every store and retail salesman in the state of Utah. His gross profit margin on each unit was $40. In all, he netted $16,000 on the Hotpoint washers, by far the hottest-selling appliance in his store.

Less than a year later, though, one of his customers called to report that the spinning cycle on her new Hotpoint washer had gradually slowed down, ultimately reaching a point where the machine was leaving clothes sopping wet.

Bill dispatched Lamar Sessions, who discovered that the spin mechanism had failed. Under the manufacturer's one-year warranty, Hotpoint provided a new part and Sessions made the repair.

Then another customer called with the same problem, followed by another. Before long, Bill was swamped with service calls for the new Hotpoint machines. By this time, he had to hire another serviceman—Lowell Hansen, a local industrial mechanic who was exceptional at diagnosing and fixing electrical appliances.

But the immensity of the Hotpoint service problem convinced Bill that he needed to change the way his business dealt with repairs. It was taking too much of his time away from sales. It made sense to separate sales from service.

He met with Sessions and Hansen. The three of them came up with an idea to have Sessions and Hansen start their own service and repair business. Bill promised to send all of the store's customer repairs to them, along with all warranty service. That would allow Bill to focus on sales and guarantee Sessions and Hansen an immediate customer base as well as an opportunity to earn more money than they were making as in-house repairmen for the store.

Eager to start his own business, Hansen readily agreed. Sessions willingly went along. He and Hansen formed S&H Repairs and began operating out of Hansen's double-wide garage.

Hansen and Sessions soon determined that Hotpoint's innovative spin mechanism—the machine's top selling point—was defective. It was only a matter of time before every machine that Bill had sold would be called in for repair. There was another problem: the replacement parts the manufacturer provided were identical to the ones that had failed. And the manufacturer's warranty only covered the original parts for one year. There was no warranty on the defective replacement parts. When those failed, R.C. Willey would be on the hook.

Bill did the math. If he got stuck paying for those parts, the combined cost of the parts and the labor to fix a Hotpoint spin mechanism would wipe out almost a full year's profit for the store.

He called the distributor again and complained.

The distributor insisted that no other retailer had called with so many complaints.

No other retailer, Bill argued, had sold so many Hotpoint washing machines.

Despite being right, Bill didn't get far. Hotpoint played hardball and insisted they would do nothing more than what the warranty required. When Bill pointed out that replacing one defective part with an identical defective part made no sense, Hotpoint ignored him.

Bill immediately stopped selling Hotpoint automatic washers and started selling another brand. The situation made him reconsider his decision to continue running the business. After two and a half years of working tirelessly to dig the business out of debt, he was finally on the brink of having a break-out year in terms of profits. The prospect of his first year of profitability evaporating due to a defective part was a depressing thought. He was simply working way too hard to only break even.

Yet he couldn't help thinking that he was capable, if given the time, of building R.C. Willey into a highly successful business. He'd already done a lot of the heavy lifting to clear the way.

There was something else making it hard for him to quit—his customers. If he closed the business, hundreds of customers who purchased the new Hotpoint machines would be left with a defective appliance.

That's not the RC Willey way, Bill thought to himself.

Knowing he'd take a loss, he decided to cover the cost to repair every washing machine that came back with a defective spin mechanism. The decision cost him thousands of dollars. But eventually Hotpoint acknowledged the defective design and released a new model. The company also issued R.C. Willey a token payment to offset some of the store's expenses.

In the meantime, Bill's generous decision to cover the cost of repairs endeared him to his customers. With service like that, people didn't want to shop anywhere else.

From the day he started selling refrigerators off the back of his pickup truck, RC Willey had always beaten his competitors by consistently offering a lower price, even if it meant foregoing profits by selling at cost.

Bill put an emphasis on low prices, too. But he was constantly on the lookout for ways to improve the store's profit margins through innovation and efficiency. It occurred to him that the store should diversify beyond just electrical appliances. Personally, he was drawn to furniture. He liked the look and feel of new sofas and beds. They also seemed to make good business sense. With no motors or moving parts, furniture required little maintenance and service once it left the store—a big plus considering what he had just gone through with Hotpoint and its faulty spin drive.

Bill also had little competition selling furniture in the North Davis County area. He approached a local manufacturer of sofas and convinced the man to sell him a few at wholesale price. When customers came to the R.C. Willey showroom to buy appliances, Bill always invited them to check out the sofas, which he stocked in his personal garage, located about fifty yards from the store. R.C. Willey already had a strong customer base. It made sense to try to sell them more products—and furniture was the ideal offering.

The sofas immediately sold out, convincing Bill that he had to create more store space to accommodate furniture. In 1957, he added 1,800 square feet to the store's original footprint of 600 square feet. To finance the addition, he used money he had acquired in a short-term real estate deal. Right after taking over the store, Bill had purchased and renovated an apartment house, which he later sold for a profit. Those proceeds paid for the construction of the store's addition, ensuring that the business didn't take on any more debt.

A bigger store and more merchandise added to the sales profits. But Bill desperately needed more help running the store.

Muscular, with curly blond hair, eighteen-year-old

Sheldon Child admired everything about his older brother—his work ethic, the fact that he was the first one in the family to obtain a college degree, and his overall leadership skills. But what he admired most was his brother's athleticism. Bill had been a standout football player and track star in high school before going on to play college sports. He was even undefeated as a boxer, at one point defeating a National Golden Glove champion.

Eager to follow in his brother's footsteps, Sheldon gave up his favorite sport—baseball—to focus on football and track. He probably would have boxed, too, if the high school hadn't dropped it as a sport during Bill's senior year of high school. Any time an opportunity arose to be around his brother, Sheldon took it.

When Bill asked Sheldon to work for him part-time, Sheldon eagerly accepted. During his final two years of high school, he had done small jobs for Bill around the store, anything that kept the place looking spotless inside and attractive outside. At night and on Saturdays he'd also helped out by answering phones, freeing Bill to make house calls on customers.

But Sheldon's biggest asset was his ability to handle customers when Bill wasn't at the store. If someone showed up wanting to see Bill, Sheldon would say that he was Bill's brother and ask if he could help them. That always worked. And very often, Sheldon would end up showing products to customers.

Even after he started his freshman year of college at Utah State in the fall of 1956, Sheldon drove home every

Friday night in order to work Saturdays. Bill had him deliver and install appliances alongside Roy Hodson, the new home deliveryman who Bill hired to replace Lamar Sessions. Big, strong, and knowledgeable when it came to electric appliances, Hodson was efficient at installing. But interacting with customers wasn't his strong suit; he rarely said a word while in a customer's home.

Sheldon was just the opposite. He thrived off explaining and demonstrating how the appliances worked. Most of the time, he and Hodson delivered washing machines. After hauling a washer down into a customer's basement, Sheldon and Hodson would position it in the desired location, level it up, hook up the water hoses, and plug it in. Then Sheldon would turn to the woman of the house.

"You're going to love this machine," he'd tell her. "It's one of the best. Let me just show you how it works so that when we leave, you can just throw your things in and not have any problem."

While the woman looked on, Sheldon guided her through a wash cycle, step by step. Along the way, he'd point out all the features from the temperature gauge to the spin cycle. His demonstration typically lasted fifteen minutes.

"Do you have any questions?" he'd ask at the end.

Typically there were none. Customers were just grateful to have such comprehensive, in-home service from a deliveryman.

"Is there anything else we can do for you?" Sheldon would ask before leaving.

The more Sheldon interacted with customers, the more

he enjoyed working for his brother. He liked it enough that he transferred from Utah State to the University of Utah after his freshman year in order to shorten his commute to work. That summer he also married Joan Haacke, his high school sweetheart. They rented RC Willey's old home, right next door to the store. The proximity allowed him to work even more hours.

Bill paid Sheldon $1.15 per hour, a sufficient income given that his tuition was covered by a scholarship. Coupled with the convenience of his commute, Sheldon had the perfect arrangement to get him through college.

Bill's decision to expand the store and beef up the furniture industry paid off immediately. In one year, sales at the store doubled. Bill quickly started buying upholstered furniture from multiple local manufacturers, adding products such as mattresses to his inventory as well. Almost overnight, the enlarged 2,400-foot showroom was too small. Furniture required a lot more floor space than appliances.

With all the new volume, he had to hire one full-time salesman and one part-time salesman. He also had no choice but to expand again. But he had no intention of putting a mortgage on the building in order to pay for construction costs. It had taken him four years to pay off the $9,000 loan that RC had taken out when he built his small warehouse. Bill had sold more than 200 electric ranges and 100 electric water heaters to make enough in rebate money through the power company's incentive program to pay off the bank.

After that experience, Bill vowed to never do anything that would encumber the company again. Instead, he called on George Wilcox, the banker he'd started doing business with a few years earlier at First National Bank. Based on Bill's impressive track record, Wilcox offered R.C. Willey an extended line of credit.

Bill ended up hardly tapping it, however. Instead, he used sales profits to pay for the expansion, enabling the building to be constructed without a mortgage. The new space called for more staff and at least one more full-time salesman. As much as Bill preferred interacting with customers on the sales floor, the growth of the company required him to delegate that responsibility to others so that he could focus his energies on managing the business. He had no intentions of repeating a mistake made by a competitor who had tried doing everything himself.

The competitor had begun operating a small furniture business out of the two-car garage adjacent to his house. Located in a residential neighborhood, the business looked and felt like the R.C. Willey store in its early days—low overhead and low prices. The owner also provided great one-on-one service, eventually hustling his way to a point where his business required a large storefront to keep up with demand. The city forced him to relocate outside of the residential area. The growth forced the owner to hire more employees to staff the store. But he failed to empower them to do their jobs. Instead, he tried to personally perform every aspect of the business, just like he did when it operated out of his home garage. As a result, customer service suffered, as did employee morale. Eventually the store couldn't sustain enough sales to keep up with the cost of the overhead, and the business went under.

His competitor's demise had taught Bill some valuable lessons. First, delegation is vital to growing a small business. Second, true delegation only exists when the leader trusts his people enough to allow them to perform their responsibilities without constant interference.

Deliveryman Roy Hodson knew Bill was on the hunt for another full-time salesman. He decided to speak up. He had watched Sheldon interact with customers every time they installed a washing machine.

"You know," Hodson told Bill, "Sheldon is tremendous. When we leave a customer's home he has those people totally sold."

Bill already had his eye on his little brother for the salesman's position. Sheldon had a great way with customers and he lived next door to the store, ensuring his ability to work long and flexible hours.

The promotion and the promise of a modest commission on top of his salary appealed to Sheldon. He was nearing the completion of his junior year of college, and he and his wife were expecting their first child. He agreed to start right away.

■ ■ ■

CHAPTER SEVEN

ALL IN THE FAMILY

February 14, 1959

It was a Saturday when Sheldon arrived at the store ready for his first official day as a salesman. Saturdays were always the busiest day of the week and he got off to a fast start—selling radios, washers, and upholstered sofas. Then he received an urgent call from his wife, who was nine months pregnant.

"I think it's time," she said.

Sheldon dropped everything and grabbed Bill. "I've got to go to the hospital," he said.

Bill eagerly sent his little brother on his way and covered for him on the showroom floor. Within a couple of hours, Sheldon's first son was born.

It was a hectic time for Sheldon, who was starting a family and going to college full-time while still helping his brother build a business. But he was up for it. Besides, the pace was only temporary. As good as he was at selling, Sheldon remained committed to teaching. With only twenty credits standing between him and a college degree, he was less than a year away from being eligible for his first job in education.

As summer wound down, he reminded Bill that the fall semester would be starting in a couple of weeks. To focus on his studies, Sheldon would have to substantially cut back his hours at the store.

Bill hoped Sheldon would stay on full-time; he was the best salesman in the store. He was also the youngest. If he stuck with it, Sheldon had the potential for a very lucrative career in the furniture business. Besides, Bill hated to see his younger brother go. The store was growing at a breakneck pace and Sheldon was an important part of the success. He decided to have a talk with him.

"Look," Bill told him, "I'm not going to tell you what to do. But if you're going to teach, then you ought to go back to school. But if you're going to stay in the furniture business, I don't think a degree will make a difference."

Sheldon felt torn. He really wanted to complete school and teach. Nature and birds had always been his passion, not sofas and mattresses. But Bill had a point. Sheldon had a gift when it came to selling. He had a wonderful knowledge of the products, superb communication skills, and a way of connecting with customers. Everyone who dealt with him trusted him. Those intangible qualities couldn't be taught.

Bill recognized the significance of the decision. He suggested taking a year to think it over. "You could spend a year working and then decide whether to go back to school," he said.

Sheldon took Bill's suggestion.

Fall 1959

Standing in wet snow as he supervised the unloading of a shipment of new appliances from a delivery truck to his warehouse, Bill spotted a familiar face rounding the corner of the store. Fay Hansen, a thirty-three-year-old mother of five sons, was a member of his church congregation. Her husband, a retired B-17 gunner who flew thirty-five combat missions in World War II, worked at a family-owned lumberyard with his brothers. Fay was looking for a job to help supplement her husband's income. She had heard that the R.C. Willey store might need some additional help.

At that time, few mothers in the greater Salt Lake City region were in the workforce. But Bill's store was less than a mile from Fay's home, and she knew enough about Bill through their association at church to trust that he'd allow her the flexibility to leave work when her children needed her at home. She asked Bill if he was hiring.

Connie O'Brien had recently stopped working, and Bill desperately needed office help and someone to oversee accounts payable. He interviewed Hansen on the spot while standing behind the store.

Hansen had a high school diploma and some work

experience as a grocery store cashier. More important, in Bill's eyes, she carried herself in a professional, dignified manner. She was bright and had a reputation for integrity and paying attention to detail.

Bill explained what he needed. With furniture now coming in by the truckload, he had a warehouse foreman to inspect all the shipments. But Bill was chewing up lots of time tracking the freight bills with the purchase orders. He needed someone to take over that responsibility and manage the office.

Hansen agreed to take on those duties.

Convinced, Bill hired her as the office manager and also put her in charge of accounts payable.

She began work right away.

Bill's decision to hire Hansen said a lot about what he looked for in his employees. Character and work ethic carried more weight than resumes. He took the same approach with each new employee he brought on board—more than anything he wanted people who were committed to customer service. In the retail business, the rest could be learned.

Bill never advertised that he was hiring. Applicants just came to him. It was plain to see that R.C. Willey was expanding. While other stores that sold furniture were cutting back, Bill was adding more and more product lines to his store. As a result, Bill picked up some of the top furniture salesmen in the area, putting them on the floor alongside Sheldon.

"We're looking for a washing machine."

Sheldon often heard that from customers as they entered the store.

"Well, there are a lot of good washing machines on the market," Sheldon would typically respond, before naming a few different brands that the store had in stock. "But if I was going to buy a washing machine today, this is the one I'd buy."

After leading them to the preferred model, he'd show them how it worked. The technique was simple and very effective. It worked largely because Sheldon focused in on the customers' needs, no matter what they were after. In order to sell the right piece of furniture, he believed, a salesman must know where the piece is going, who will use it, and what kind of use it will get.

When someone came in looking for a new sofa, Sheldon would respond with a question: "Where are you going to use it?"

Then he'd ask how many children lived in the customer's home. Finally, he'd determine whether the sofa would receive hard use or soft use. Selling radios and stereos was much different. Electronics served a different function than furniture or appliances. When Bill first introduced stereos as a product line in the R.C. Willey store, Sheldon fell in love with a Motorola unit that featured a record player and an AM/FM radio with built-in speakers in a wood-faced cabinet. Since he had bought one himself, he had instant credibility when he told customers how well the unit performed.

Before he knew it, Sheldon had been selling furniture

and appliances for more than a year. His clientele was growing as customers kept recommending him to their friends and relatives. His sales pitch just didn't feel like a pitch. Rather, he made people feel at home, which was exactly the feeling Bill wanted R.C. Willey customers to have.

The store's success had a snowball effect. By word of mouth, more and more customers were coming into the store. Bill was hiring more men to join the sales force. And Sheldon's income increased as his commissions rose. It was pretty clear that business wasn't slowing down.

Sheldon and his wife recognized he wasn't going back to school anytime soon. Instead, they broke ground on their first home, building it next door to Bill's house.

As more and more customers traded in old appliances for new ones, Bill acquired quite an inventory of used merchandise, storing the items in the warehouse. The demand for used appliances was strong enough that Bill wanted to offer those to customers who couldn't afford new ones. Before long, he started acquiring used furniture, too. But he simply didn't have time to devote to that aspect of the business. Neither did Sheldon.

The two brothers talked about what to do. Together they came up with a possible solution: "Let's hire Dad."

Born in 1901 in Hooper, Utah, Fay Child had taught Bill and Sheldon everything they knew about hard work, integrity, and ambition. When the boys were young, their father was always working. Besides running the family farm, he maintained a part-time job on the side to bring in extra money. But Fay was getting older, and farm work was becoming too demanding for him.

When Bill offered him a job selling used appliances and furniture, Fay gave an immediate response: "I'd love to."

Buying and selling used merchandise is a lot like horse trading—it requires a certain savvy and mentality. Fay was an ideal candidate since he had traded horses and cattle for nearly fifty years as one of the primary aspects of his farming operation. His experience proved to be essential almost immediately after he began working at the store. One day, a man named Al DeCorso approached him about buying large quantities of R.C. Willey's inventory of used furniture and appliances.

DeCorso ran a used appliance and furniture store in Ogden. He typically paid for everything in cash, and he was skilled at obtaining furniture for next to nothing in order to turn a profit when he resold it in his shop. Fay jokingly nicknamed him Jessie James.

Fay and DeCorso spent hours haggling over prices, ultimately coming to agreements that suited both sides. Fay knew how to handle DeCorso and the two men became friends. Bill soon expanded his father's responsibilities to include handling returned goods and damaged furniture.

"I loved having Dad there," Sheldon said. "It was great to see how much fun he was having at the store. And he was very good at what he was doing. Plus, it is always good to be with your dad."

April 1964

Fast approaching the ten-year anniversary of the day he took over the store, Bill constantly retooled the business to anticipate consumption trends. With so many people buying upholstered goods, he undertook another expansion to make way for more furniture. This time he added 24,000 square feet to the showroom, making it the largest furniture store outside Salt Lake City. He even changed the name to R.C. Willey Furniture and Appliance Store.

Selling furniture was more profitable than selling appliances. But that wasn't the only reason Bill moved his inventory in that direction. He already had a loyal customer base, and his goal was simply to sell home furnishing items to the same people who had bought appliances. "The first year we added furniture, our overall sales volume in the store doubled," Bill said. "That's because we were selling more product to the same customers."

For Bill it was all about understanding his customers. Conventional wisdom suggested that a rural cornfield wasn't the ideal place to begin building a thriving retail business. And it wasn't. But Bill had turned the unconventional location into an advantage, using advertising slogans such as, "Drive to the country and save," and, "Lower overhead means lower prices because of our country location." By human nature, people like to find a bargain. Traveling to Syracuse for high quality at a lower price became the thing to do. Before long, the store's bargain-friendly image took hold and began to set the company apart from all of its competitors.

"Starting a business in a cornfield is sort of like being handed a lemon," Bill said. "But we took what we were given and converted it into lemonade. The fact that we began with a small building that had no rent and low overhead enabled us to get off on the right foot."

R.C. Willey's look and feel was also a perfect match for the demographic profile of its customer base. In the 1960s, more than ninety-five percent of the residents in Syracuse belonged to the Mormon faith, which stresses the importance of the family and what goes on in the home. All of the surrounding communities were predominantly Mormon, too.

"The home is the focal point of our lives here," Bill told a leading furniture industry publication. "An emphasis on home furnishings naturally follows."

To establish his store as the premier home furnishings venue in the state, Bill looked outside Utah for his merchandise. He made regular trips to San Francisco and the East Coast to inspect and acquire top furniture lines from around the world. While Bill traveled and rubbed shoulders with leading wholesalers and manufacturers, Sheldon and seven other full-time salesmen sold anything and everything Bill put on the showroom floor.

In all, Bill had a staff of fifty full-time employees. It was a totally different approach than RC took when he ran the business. Unsurpassed as a salesman, RC had mastered the technique of placing appliances in customers' homes on a free trial basis. This was just one of his ingenious ways of getting people to buy. But he never hired or trained others to replicate his approach, limiting his profits to what he could personally generate.

RC had also chosen to do every other aspect of the business himself, taking time away from what he did best—selling. Bill, on the other hand, believed in delegation. Rather than micromanaging every aspect of the store, he hired competent people to sell, deliver, keep the books and handle credit collection, and to manage accounts receivable, accounts payable, and customer service. This approach allowed him to focus on his strengths: managing the business, buying products, hiring employees, and planning for future development. Always with an eye toward new products and store expansion, Bill continually diversified the store, creating an ever-changing experience when shoppers entered R.C. Willey. It didn't take long before it became a one-stop shopping spot for everything needed to furnish a home, from furniture and appliances to lighting and carpeting.

In the spring of 1965, Bill's wife, Darline, slipped and fell, badly bruising her leg. When the pain hadn't receded after a few days, a doctor prescribed a common blood-thinning medication. A couple nights later, Bill received a frantic call at the store. Darline's leg had swelled up immensely and the pain was unbearable.

Bill rushed her to the hospital, where doctors determined Darline had developed a blood clot in her leg. But they couldn't figure out the cause. Nor could doctors stop the clotting. Darline was hospitalized for nearly three months, undergoing a series of experimental treatments. The doctors concluded that she had a rare condition that predisposed her to blood clots, and in August, Darline died at age 31. She and Bill had been married eleven years and had four children, two boys and two girls.

Darline's fall and hospitalization had happened so abruptly and the pain from her absence left Bill feeling as if his own life had ended. His best friend was gone, and his children didn't understand what had happened. Bill's parents were also heartbroken—they were deeply fond of Darline, and her premature passing left a big void in their lives as well.

The extended family did all it could to rally around Bill and his children. Darline's mother had remained at her daughter's bedside throughout the ordeal. After the funeral, she continued to assume a lot of responsibility around Bill's home. Sheldon and his wife also came to Bill's aid. Living next door, they were able to help out with meals and childcare. Bill's two daughters even lived at Sheldon's for awhile, and Joan treated them as if they were her own—doing their hair every morning before ushering them off to school. Additionally, Bill's mother and sister were at his house daily.

"It was a blessing to have Sheldon and Joan next door," Bill said. "It's hard to imagine what it would have been like trying to go through that tragedy without our family at our side."

Meanwhile, Darline's Aunt June moved into Bill's house right after Darline's passing. She took over all childcare, housecleaning, and cooking responsibilities Monday through

Friday. A widow, Aunt June had helped raise Darline after Darline's older sister became very ill during early childhood.

Bill could have easily neglected the business or elected to give up on it altogether. Instead, he found strength in his faith. Mormons believe that families reunite in heaven. This belief helped ease Bill's pain. Nights and weekends were devoted to his children; weekdays were consumed with trying to stay on top of his fast-growing business. Bill was so busy he didn't have time to think, which proved to be a good thing. Depression didn't have time to take hold while his mind was so preoccupied.

CHAPTER EIGHT

■ ■ ■

NEVER ON SUNDAY

Utah is the only state that celebrates Pioneer Day, a holiday held on July 24th that honors the Mormon pioneers and their historic trek from the eastern states to the Salt Lake Valley. State and local government offices, banks, and most businesses shut down for the day. But after taking over the R.C. Willey store from his father-in-law, Bill found it near impossible to avoid working on Pioneer Day, despite the fact that the store was officially closed. Inevitably, since other states didn't celebrate the holiday, truckers hauling furniture from North Carolina to California would show up at the store on Pioneer Day to deliver merchandise. Finding the store locked, drivers would end up at Bill's home, which was across the street, asking him to unlock the building and receive the load. Otherwise, the trucker would be forced to lay over in Salt Lake City for a full day.

As soon as Bill unlocked the store to help unload freight, the telephone would start ringing and customers would begin pulling up to the store expecting to shop. It was apparent that customers wanted to buy furniture and appliances on holidays. R.C. Willey was already open on Memorial Day. Bill had made that decision one year after going to the store on a rainy Memorial Day to do some paperwork. That day he couldn't answer the phone fast enough, repeatedly fielding calls from customers asking if the store was open. Bill also saw dozens of cars drive up to the store that day, only to drive away after realizing the place was closed.

Determined to listen and respond to his customers, Bill decided to break with tradition and open the store on Pioneer Day too. Initially, the sales force, who were predominantly Mormon, complained. But the complaints ended when business proved to be so exceptional on Pioneer Day that the sales team made better-than-average commissions. To increase sales volume even more, Bill promoted Pioneer Day with big, one-day sales, along with free hot dogs and beverages for all customers. Pioneer Day quickly became as popular of a shopping day as Memorial Day.

Soon R.C. Willey opened on other holidays, offering big sales, complimentary in-store gifts, and free food. As was the case with Pioneer Day, the other holidays were among the most successful days the store had each year. As R.C. Willey remained open on more and more holidays, some employees complained. But holidays proved to be a very popular day for customers to shop. And with its competitors also open for business on holidays, R.C. Willey couldn't afford to turn all that business away by remaining closed.

To mollify his employees, Bill reminded them that they always got Sundays off. Unlike many other stores, R.C. Willey never opened on Sunday. Even when national furniture chains and department stores entered the Utah market and opened for business on Sunday, Bill and Sheldon resisted. The majority of R.C. Willey's employees and customers were Mormons, who believe that Sundays should be a day dedicated to faith and to family.

Besides remaining closed on Sundays, R.C. Willey made another pivotal decision—turning to television for advertising. In the 1960s, very few furniture and appliance stores in Utah made television commercials. The medium was still relatively new and most stores couldn't afford the advertising cost. But Bill recognized TV as a powerful way to reach new customers all over Utah. He started buying a few spots on all three local network affiliates. Almost immediately, LeGrand Young, the account executive from KSL who handled advertising sales, started dropping by the store on a weekly basis to see Bill in an attempt to persuade him to buy more television spots. KSL enjoyed the largest viewership of the three network stations.

Bill had been paying close attention to KSL's television commercials and had observed that they had a number of prime-time slots filled by advertisements for KSL programming. He couldn't imagine why the station would waste valuable prime-time spots promoting television shows, convincing him that the station must have failed to sell those spots to companies or businesses. That got him thinking.

A television advertisement spot is a lot like a seat on an airplane. Even if a commercial jet has a few empty seats, the plane still takes off. But the airline loses revenue on the unsold seats. Television stations are in the same predicament. The shows must go on whether or not all the ad spots are sold. The next time Bill met with Young, he asked a question: "What happens if the station has ad spots that aren't sold?"

Young explained that the revenue would be lost, confirming what Bill had thought—television ad spots were perishable. So he made Young an offer: R.C. Willey would pay $50 for every unsold spot that normally went for anywhere from $250 to more than $1,000. The prices were predicated on the audience levels. The proposal guaranteed that the station would collect at least some revenue for every advertisement slot that would otherwise generate no revenue for the station.

KSL accepted Bill's proposal, and R.C. Willey started airing a lot more commercials, including some that ran during the evening news and prime-time programming hours on weeknights. The exposure established R.C. Willey all over the state, but particularly in the Salt Lake City market. R.C. Willey's competitors couldn't figure out how Bill could afford to advertise on television so much.

Meanwhile, Bill identified the perfect person to introduce Wasatch Front viewers to R.C. Willey: Ray LeBreck, a middle-aged employee who began working in the credit department at R.C. Willey during the early 1960s. LeBreck had no experience making commercials, nor did he look like a polished actor or sound like a professional spokesman. Instead, he came across as what he was—a Utah native who simply loved his job and had a great way with people. Bill was impressed with his contagious smile and the way he put people at ease. There was nothing pushy or staged about him.

LeBreck became the store's informal spokesman and a television personality throughout northern Utah, appearing in many different commercials. But all of them ended with the same words: "Come save money with us. But never on Sunday." Clever and subtle, the slogan "Never on Sunday" played over and over on television, effectively branding R.C. Willey as the hometown store with hometown values.

People became so used to seeing LeBreck on television that Bill decided to use him as a store greeter in addition to his television work. LeBreck would shake customers' hands and welcome them to R.C. Willey. Customers got a kick out of meeting him and the store's image continued to improve.

CHAPTER NINE

■ ■ ■

TAKE THE LONG VIEW

A primary reason that R.C. Willey Home Furnishings maintained such strong sales growth year in and year out was the store's close proximity to Hill Air Force Base, which was located just under ten miles from R.C. Willey. At one point during World War II, the base employed more than 20,000 civilians and 3,000 military personnel responsible for supplying and maintaining many of the aircraft used in combat over Europe and the Pacific. During the Korean War, the base handled a major portion of the Air Force's logistical effort—renovating planes and keeping the aircraft inventory active. And as the United States settled into the Cold War with Russia, the base became a critical maintenance support hub for a host of military jets and missile delivery systems.

By far the biggest employer in either Davis or Weber counties, the base had a tremendous impact on the local economy. Retail stores, in particular, benefited from the military presence. By the mid-1960s, Bill calculated that about sixty-five percent of R.C. Willey's sales were generated by people employed at the base. When it came to furniture, active-duty military personnel were particularly reliable customers; enlisted men would buy furniture when they first arrived in the area. Since transfers were frequent, there was a steady influx of new personnel needing home furnishings. Better still, it wasn't uncommon for outgoing enlisted men to return to Hill Air Force Base after a tour of duty elsewhere in the world, resulting in returning R.C. Willey customers who were already familiar with the company's name.

With the base providing such a boon to the economy, Bill figured it was the ideal time to plan for a downturn. Rumors were always circulating that the Department of Defense might dramatically scale back the base and its personnel, a move that would surely have a debilitating impact on area businesses. The rumors had yet to materialize; nonetheless, Bill didn't like being so reliant on the military. He decided to diversify. That meant expanding the store's customer base.

With the television advertising campaign elevating R.C. Willey's name recognition throughout the Salt Lake City region, Bill wanted to take the next step and open a store there. Not only was the region responsible for about half of the state's economy but it also wasn't dependent on military-based employment. The store's potential for success there seemed limitless.

Where, exactly, to build in Salt Lake City required more forethought. Bill started looking for sites.

While Bill was focusing on expanding his business, his personal life took a turn for the better. Twenty-six-year-old Patricia Wright worked as a medical technician at a Salt Lake City hospital. In January 1966, she received a call from a trusted friend whose husband was a sales representative for a mattress manufacturer. The woman explained that her husband was hosting a private dinner for a group of the top mattress dealers. All but one of the dealers would be accompanied by his spouse. Wright's friend asked her if she'd be willing to attend the dinner with the one dealer who was single. All Wright knew was that the man was from Syracuse.

Wright assumed the man was from Syracuse, New York; she had never heard of Syracuse, Utah. Typically not fond of blind dates, Wright nonetheless agreed to her friend's request, figuring it might be interesting to meet a man from New York. When she arrived and met Bill, Wright was embarrassed to discover he lived in a small farming community twenty-five miles north of Salt Lake City. But he was charming and extremely polite. She also discovered that they shared some common interests and beliefs, not the least of which included their membership in the Mormon church.

Amongst her girlfriends, Wright had vowed there were three things she would never do. The first was marry a man who had previously been married. If, for some reason, she made an exception to rule number one, she would definitely not marry a previously married man who had children. Third, she'd never live in a small town.

On their third date, Bill took Patricia to dinner near Salt Lake City. Afterward, he invited her to ride with him to Syracuse to meet his children. Once they got off the freeway and closer to Bill's home, there were acres of farm fields and very few streetlights. Patricia wondered where on earth Bill was taking her.

But after meeting the family and spending more time with Bill, Patricia realized she was going to end up violating all three of her personal rules. On October 10, 1966, Bill and Patricia married, and she relocated to Syracuse.

Meanwhile, Bill continued to expand his business. Around the time that Bill began exploring the possibility of opening a store in Salt Lake City, he was approached by Bob Wilding, manager of a small Magnavox Home Entertainment Center franchise in Salt Lake. Convinced that an R.C. Willey store would thrive near Salt Lake City, Wilding volunteered to manage it. With Bill's permission, he started looking for potential sites. Eventually, Wilding introduced Bill to a man selling a four-acre parcel in the suburb of Murray, about ten blocks south of the city line. The parcel was part of an old farm and was situated in a more residential area, away from other stores and industry. The site suited Bill just fine; he had wanted a store site with a more rural feel to it, but he also wanted proximity to a major highway, insuring easy access to customers from all around the city. It turned out that the four-acre lot sat right along the pathway of the new beltway the state was planning to build around

Salt Lake City. The owner agreed to sell the land to Bill at an affordable price.

Convinced that he had found an ideal location at a fair price, Bill now considered the risks of going forward. For starters, there was no guarantee that an R.C. Willey store would succeed in the Salt Lake City market, even though the store had a great following twenty-five miles north of the city, in rural Davis and Weber counties. Consumers in Salt Lake may have seen R.C. Willey ads on television, but most viewers had never stepped foot in the Syracuse store. Meanwhile, there were a number of large, more established furniture stores operating in and around Salt Lake City. Bill wondered, *What if I build a new store and customers don't come?*

There were other questions to consider. Would the business be able to control expenses? Two-thirds of the expenses in a retail furniture operation stem from labor costs. New employees also needed to be trained and managed to perform as efficiently as the employees at the Syracuse store. Trying to run a store from a remote location posed a number of operational challenges that Bill had never had to consider before. Controlling inventory, delegating responsibilities, and finding good management for the new store were all issues Bill would have to tackle.

But ultimately, he figured the success of a second store all boiled down to volume. Sales solve a lot of problems. And Bill knew his business provided great value at an affordable price. He'd just have to assume the risk. "A company always goes at risk when it expands," he later said.

"But if you have done your homework and have a competitive advantage, the risk is minimized."

Rather than saddle the business with debt, Bill decided to buy the land and finance the construction of the store with his own funds. Once the store was open, Bill would lease the land and the store to the business.

After finalizing his business plan, Bill approached banker George Wilcox and requested that his credit line be increased to $300,000. Wilcox asked Bill what he had in mind. Bill outlined his expansion plans. The relationship and track record Bill had built up with Wilcox and his bank paid off. After asking a few questions, Wilcox agreed to increase Bill's credit line. He was impressed by the fact that Bill was personally assuming the risk on the land and the building—providing a strong incentive for him to perform and succeed.

Shortly after the credit line funds became available, R.C. Willey broke ground in Murray.

Every time that Bill reached a point in his career where he felt he'd finally be able to slow down a bit, he found himself working a little longer and harder each day. The year 1969 was no exception. His and Patricia's first child turned one the year that R.C. Willey opened its 20,000 square-foot store in Murray. That left virtually no time for leisure and little time for sleep. With the Syracuse store less than a hundred yards from his doorstep, Bill would run home for dinner and run back to the store right afterwards, often working past dark.

"We didn't have a lot of spare time," Patricia said. "Bill

was running one store and building another. We had older children at home who weren't quite old enough to get a driver's license so I was driving them everywhere, plus we had a new baby. It was a very hectic time, but we didn't have a lot of choice. Bill was building a business and we had a growing family; there were great demands on his time and mine."

Bill's boyhood on a farm shaped his work habits. "Growing up I learned that grain had to be cut when it was ready or the wind would come and break off the head," he said. "The alfalfa had to be put up before the rain came. Tomatoes left on the vine too long would spoil. So when it came to the business, I was willing to work however many hours it took to make it successful."

Before the Murray store opened, Bill had set a goal to make the store profitable within ninety days of the grand opening. That meant completing enough sales to cover all the grand opening expenses, along with the overhead costs, including advertising and salaries for all employees.

Within three months, the Murray store hit its earnings target. Over the next ten years, the store underwent eight expansions, and the number of employees jumped from twenty to more than two hundred.

The decision to open the new store paid off in other ways, too. Shortly after the Murray store opened, Hill Air Force Base started downsizing. Over a ten-year period, the Pentagon dramatically cut back the number of personnel on the base. But because of Bill's foresight, R.C. Willey didn't suffer a drop in its business.

■ ■ ■

CHAPTER TEN

RULES TO LIVE BY

When Bill first started working alongside RC, his father-in-law had a simple formula for success in business: *Identify a need and fill it.*

RC's approach grew out of his entrepreneurial mindset. "Customers don't really know what they want," RC used to say. "So you can tell them what they want and convince them. Once they have it, they'll appreciate it."

New inventions are a perfect example. Consider the cell phone. A consumer doesn't know he can't get by without one until he has one.

In RC's day, electric appliances were the new thing. People didn't know what it meant to have automatic washing machines, home refrigerators, and televisions. But as each of these items came on the market, RC eagerly introduced his customers to them.

For Bill and Sheldon, the challenge was finding ways to constantly expand their product lines and retain their customer base in a market that offers consumers so many choices for acquiring merchandise. Along the way, they developed some simple rules and keys to success, and they found ways to inspire their employees to adopt these core philosophies.

1. Treat every customer the way you want to be treated.

"Every company has to have rules," Bill said. "Our rule was pretty broad: Take care of the customer. Treat them as you'd like to be treated." It's simple. Yet many companies ignore this approach, caught up in enforcing policies that don't enhance the bottom line.

"If we had made an error or failed to meet a commitment," Bill recalled, "I felt it was necessary to go to any extent to satisfy the customer."

With Bill and Sheldon so committed to customer service, R.C. Willey employees went out of their way to follow their example. But occasionally a customer wasn't satisfied with the store's approach and the complaint would be heard up the chain to Bill or Sheldon. "If we felt the customer was right, we usually took the customer's side pretty quickly," Bill said. "We had to be cautious and tactful in doing that so we didn't undermine our customer service people. So it was a framing issue. But our philosophy was that you never win when you have a standoff with the customer."

That policy meant there would be instances when the store would take a loss in order to appease a consumer. "If that's the case," Bill said, "you are better off to let them take advantage of you, consequently allowing you to use your time more productively."

Shortly after Bill took over the store, R.C. Willey sold a washer and dryer to a customer who insisted on having it installed. Normally, the store provided in-home hookup service on new appliances, but the store did not do installations, a more in-depth process that often required plumbing and electrical services.

The customer assured his salesman that the plumbing and electrical supplies in his basement were close to where the washer and dryer would sit. Anxious to make the sale, R.C. Willey agreed to do the installation. But when the delivery team got to the customer's home, they discovered that the installation required a lot of work. The hot and cold water lines for the washer were actually on the opposite side of the house. A water drain had to be installed. And 220-volt wire had to be run to accommodate the dryer—which had no vent. Plumbing and electrical fees to complete these services would run about $800. The total sale on the two appliances amounted to just $400.

The store tried to convince the customer that it wasn't R.C. Willey's responsibility to do in-home plumbing and wiring. But the customer insisted they honor their agreement. Ultimately, the store agreed to do the service. "It was an $800 lesson learned," Bill said. "From that day on, all salesmen were very explicit in outlining the fact that our obligation extended to hooking up to existing plumbing and electrical."

Many businesses refuse to budge when a customer insists on a price adjustment or a refund, knowing that nine times out of ten the business will prevail over the customer. "You might convince the customer you are right," Bill said. "But then he never buys from you again. Worse still, he tells his family and friends, and you end up losing a lot more than one customer. So in the end you win the individual battle with the customer but lose the war."

Because consumers are faced with so many choices today, businesses can't afford to lose a customer over a dispute, knowing that one disgruntled customer can poison a whole neighborhood or family of customers. "Snuffing out these problems early is a little like dealing with a fire," Bill said. "If you catch it in the beginning, you can save a building.

"We have customers who have done business with us for three or four generations," Bill said. "The formula for protecting that loyalty is combining excellent customer service with the best value on quality home furnishings."

2. Little things make all the difference.

It's not uncommon to see an R.C. Willey delivery truck parked alongside a road while two deliverymen assist a stranded motorist with a flat tire or dead battery. The effort might make for an occasional late delivery, but Bill and Sheldon didn't mind; they liked the sight of a company employee providing service to members of the community. "It may cost a little to stop and help someone," Bill said, "but it's the appropriate thing to do."

These days, taking time out to help a stranger easily gives way to expediency. And in business, the appropriate thing often takes a backseat to doing what's most profitable. But the success of R.C. Willey rests on a corporate mindset that the cost of extending little courtesies is minimal, while the return at the bottom line adds up over the long run. Something as simple as making sure restrooms are always clean and well-fragranced can leave a positive impression on a customer. It's a small gesture, but nothing turns off a customer—especially a parent with a child in tow—faster than a restroom that is dirty and foul.

Similarly, Bill put a big emphasis on keeping sidewalks clean, maintaining wastebaskets in appropriate areas, and teaching employees to smile and show appreciation as customers enter and exit the store. "It doesn't cost a thing to smile or say hello when you walk past someone," he pointed out.

Besides verbally expressing appreciation, R.C. Willey employees showed they cared by routinely giving customers a complimentary gift as they entered the store. Tape measures, yardsticks, and a variety of small household items are among the inexpensive accessories that occupied the homes of many R.C. Willey customers, courtesy of the store. And on the busiest shopping days, the store would routinely arrange for free hot dogs to be served.

The courtesy gifts and parking lot barbecues helped create a festive shopping atmosphere, one that distinguished R.C. Willey stores from other furniture and appliance retailers. "These little things are details that often make the difference between success and failure," Bill said. "You don't have to do extraordinary things to get extraordinary results."

A service manager at the store once turned a little gesture into a big opportunity. One day a customer bought a bicycle at R.C. Willey. Shortly after making the purchase, the customer returned, reporting he had hit a tree. The fork on the bike was badly bent. He asked for a replacement.

The sales representative decided to replace the bike with a new one. When the service manager found out, he commended the salesman and came up with an idea to motivate other employees—he created the Golden Fork Award. It was given out monthly to the employee who did something exceptional for a customer or another employee. This created a competitive environment where employees went out of their way to improve their customer service.

3. Be honest.

Sales was one area that Bill delegated to Sheldon, who was the best sales representative in the company's history, making him the perfect person to train others. To Sheldon, sales was the key to any retail store's success. "Nothing happens until something is sold," Sheldon said. "You can have the best management in the world, but if you don't make the sales, you won't be successful."

From the day that Bill and Sheldon set out to add more members to their sales force, they made a point to look for candidates with integrity and a commitment to customer satisfaction.

"One of the things we learned," Sheldon said, "is that sales people will embellish the truth a little bit. We had a motto: 'If you always tell the truth, you never have to remember what you said.' That was something we stressed."

The motto is particularly useful in the retail furniture and appliance business. It is not unusual for a customer to come into a store and talk to a salesman about a product and then return a week or so later. "If you don't tell the truth," Sheldon said, "you can't remember what you told that customer when he comes back. So just tell the truth the first time and later you won't have to try to remember what you said."

4. Do the right thing.

By the early 1970s, R.C. Willey had begun offering extended warranties on appliances and electronics. Manufacturers typically provided a standard ninety-day or one-year warranty. For an additional cost, R.C. Willey would guarantee the product for a year or two longer. If, for example, a television failed during the extended warranty period, R.C. Willey was obligated to repair or replace it at no cost to the customer.

Eventually, R.C. Willey started selling the extended warranties to a third-party insurer that assumed responsibility for any merchandise failures covered under the extended warranty. It worked like this: R.C. Willey would sell an extended warranty to a customer for, say, $100. The store would then pay $75 to an insurer, who assumed responsibility for the cost of any repairs or replacement. This netted R.C. Willey $25 on the warranty sale, while passing on the obligation to a third party.

Under this scenario, if a customer contacted R.C. Willey and requested service under the extended warranty plan, the store would dispatch an independent technician, who would then charge the warranty insurer for the repair work. By the 1980s, R.C. Willey was selling large numbers of extended warranties, satisfying customers' requests for extended service protection.

One day Bill learned that his outside service technicians had not been paid for a large number of extended warranty repairs that had been billed to the third-party insurer. Concerned that the insurer was in financial trouble, Bill sent his chief financial officer to check on the financial stability of Electric Warranty Corporation (EWC), a national company headquartered in Oklahoma City. R.C. Willey was prepared to send EWC $193,000 in new extended warranty funds, but Bill didn't want to send the check for the warranties if the company was no longer reliable.

R.C. Willey's CFO came back from Oklahoma City and reported that he thought the company was sound. And EWC immediately paid all of its outstanding fees to R.C.

RC Willey and his wife, Helen

The Willey home in Syracuse, Utah

The original R. C. Willey store in Syracuse, Utah

RC at the original R. C. Willey Store

RC visits with a Utah Power and Light employee

Letter from Dick Gailey to Bill Child congratulating
him on paying off the mortgage

A newspaper ad announcing the first expansion
to the R. C. Willey store

Bill Child's first business card

Bill Child and Lowell Hansen, who managed the
appliance department with Lamar Sessions

Bill Child (right) and his brother, Sheldon Child (left)

Bill Child's parents, Viola and Fay

WEEKLY REFLEX, DAVIS NEWS JOURNAL, Thursday, August, 19, 1965

Young Matron Dies After Long Illness

Mrs. Helen Darline Willey Child, 31, died Saturday evening at the LDS hospital in Salt Lake, after an illness of the past five months.

SHE WAS born on Aug. 8, 1934, in Ogden, a daughter of Rufus C. and Helen Swaner Willey. She was married to William H. Child, who is general manager of the R. C. Willey Furniture and Appliance Store in Syracuse, on June 1, 1951 in the Salt Lake LDS Temple.

Mrs. Child has been very active in the Syracuse 2nd LDS ward, having served in the Primary Association, as a teacher, an organist, and served as president for three years. She had also been a teacher in the MIA for a number of years.

MRS. CHILD was a 4-H club leader; had been president of the Syracuse Elementary PTA; and was a member of the Iris Camp, Daughters of Utah Pioneers. At the time of her death she was organist in the DUP Camp.

Surviving are her husband, two sons and two daughters. William Steven,

Mrs. Darline W. Child

David R., Shauna D. and Nancy Ann Child, all of Syracuse; her mother, Mrs. Helen Willey Barber, and her stepfather, Clyde Barber, Syracuse; one brother, and one sister, Dr. Darrell S. Willey, Las Cruces, N. M. and Mrs. Bette W. McBroom, Upland, Calif.; also two step-brothers, and two step-sisters, J. Vaun Barber, Rex C. Barber, and Mrs. Dick (Shirley) Egan, Syracuse; and Mrs. H. H. (Irene) Holland, Burley, Ida.   vb

PROGRAM for the funeral services were as follows:

Family prayer, Patriarch Lawrence I. Criddle; invocation, Dale T. Smedley; prelude and postlude organ music, Mrs. Alice O. Gailey; opening musical selection and reading, by Mrs. Iola Murray, accompanied by Mrs. Gailey; speaker, J. Vaun Barber.

SPEAKER, Pres. George S. Reid; vocal solo, "That Wonderful Mother of Mine," by Warren G. Bennett; speaker, Bishop C. Russell Hansen; vocal duet, "I'll Walk With God," by Mrs. Maxine S. Smedley and Dick Egan; benediction by Sheldon Child.

Dedication of the grave in the Syracuse city cemetery, by Dr. Darrell S. Willey, brother of Mrs. Child. Mrs. Gailey accompanied all the vocalists.

PALLBEARERS were Don Willey, Lynn Wood, Norman Hansen, Rex Thurgood, Glen Willey, Don Thorpe, Harvey Peterson and Rudell Willey.

The Syracuse 2nd LDS ward Relief Society was in charge of the flowers.

FUNERAL services were conducted Wednesday at the North Davis Stake Center, Syracuse, with Bishop Ferrall S. Gailey conducting.

Mrs. Child was taken ill the first part of last March, and has been confined to the hospital for more than four months. She underwent numerous operations during this time.

Helen Darline Willey Child

Date of Death August 14, 1965

Obituary notice for Helen Child

Bill Child and his father, Fay, late 1980s

Bill Child with his wife, Patricia, and his mother, Viola, aged 103, 2006

R. C. Willey store in Murray, Utah

R. C. Willey Corporate Offices and showroom, South Salt Lake, Utah

An original painting by Wyland adorns the side of R. C. Willey Corporate offices

R. C. Willey store in Boise, Idaho

R. C. Willey continued to expand as the company continued to be successful

Bill believed in decorating the store to look like a home

Bill Child at the groundbreaking ceremony for the Boise, Idaho, store

Left to right: Irv Blumkin, Warren Buffett, Bill Child, Louie Blumkin

Warren visits the Orem store for the first time
Left to right: David Child, Warren Buffett, Bill Child, Sheldon Child

Warren Buffett visited the R. C. Willey Stores
before deciding to make an offer

Warren Buffett and Bill Child attend a
Grand Opening of an R. C. Willey Store

Bill and his wife pose in front of a display at the
Davis Applied Technology College

R. C. Willey store in Summerlin, Nevada

Customers line up for the grand opening of the Summerlin store in Nevada

An illustration by Steve Kropp of Warren Buffett and Bill Child that
appeared in the February 1997 issue of *Utah Business*

Bill Child's invitation to the Alfalfa Club

A Christmas card from
Warren Buffett to Bill Child

Bill Child and Warren Buffett

Warren Buffett spends some time with young business school students

A casual lunch between friends, January 2009

Warren Buffett shows his support of the University of Utah
win in the 2005 Fiesta Bowl

Warren Buffett and Bill Child—
friends and colleagues

Warren Buffett handing over his
wallet to Bill Child

Bill Child, his wife, Patricia, and Warren Buffett, 2005

Bill Child and Warren Buffett, 2005

On a buying trip to China: (left to right) Bill Child, tour guide,
Sue Green, Jeff Child, Brenda Hoskins

Playing golf at Augusta National Golf Course: (left to right) Bill Child,
Jeff Rakes, Warren Buffett, and Bill Gates

Bill Child, 2006, just prior to leaving for his two-year mission
for The Church of Jesus Christ of Latter-day Saints

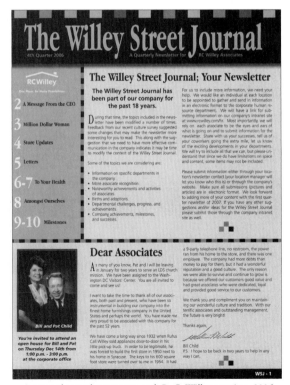

A quarterly newsletter sent to each R. C. Willey associate, 2006

Willey's outside service technicians. At that point, R.C. Willey released a $193,000 check for warranty fees. Four days later, the insurer declared bankruptcy, which made the national news.

Bill had a decision to make. Legally, he was not responsible for the warranties—the obligations rested with the bankrupt company—so he could essentially tell customers, "Sorry, you're out of luck." In fact, that's what some other retailers affiliated with EWC did.

But a business reporter from a Salt Lake City television station was familiar with R.C. Willey's long-standing reputation for customer satisfaction and tracked Bill down and asked him how R.C. Willey planned to handle the matter. Bill told the reporter that the store would step in and honor the warranties on any products purchased in an R.C. Willey store. Customers had bought the extended warranties in good faith and R.C. Willey planned to honor them in good faith.

"Will you say that on TV?" the reporter asked.

Not eager to be on television, Bill nonetheless said he would. His approach was controversial and drew a lot of attention. Over the ensuing five years, R.C. Willey spent $1.5 million honoring extended warranties. "We felt it was the right thing to do," Bill said. "Customers trust us enough to purchase products from us. So we felt that we should cover the guarantees."

5. Don't follow the herd.

In 1975, R.C. Willey became one of the first retailers in the furniture industry to issue its own personal credit cards on a major scale. The move was particularly bold in light of the fact that the industry trend at that time was moving away from in-house financing altogether. "A lot of companies didn't have the financial strength to venture into the business of financing," Bill said. "It took capital and it could be risky. But we saw it as another opportunity to build our brand."

The experiment of direct financing to customers ended up being a smart business move on a number of levels. First, R.C. Willey increased its profitability prospects. Typically, when retailers sell merchandise on credit, they transfer the credit account to a third-party lender, such as a bank or credit card company. Those lending institutions charge high interest rates and assess steep penalties for late or missed payments. By self-financing, R.C. Willey eliminated the third-party lender, enabling the store to charge lower interest rates to customers while retaining all the profits generated through interest payments.

This move guaranteed that R.C. Willey would have more control over a customer's overall purchasing experience, a business principle known as "vertical control"— referring to a customer's entire purchasing experience from top to bottom. The store already controlled the customer's purchase experience by handling the on-the-floor sale. The store also controlled the delivery and installation of merchandise, as well as the service or maintenance aspect of the transaction. But the store had no control over what happened to customers who purchased on credit and therefore had to deal with an outside lender.

"When we turn a customer over to a financial company, we don't know how harsh they'll be with the customer," Bill said. "We knew that we could be more compassionate or understanding if a monthly installment payment were missed due to a person losing his job, experiencing a sudden illness, or encountering some other unforeseen circumstance. We were better equipped than an outside, impersonal company when it came to meeting individual customer needs. We took a personal interest in our customer's long-term satisfaction."

Meanwhile, more and more consumers were walking around with an R.C. Willey credit card in their wallet. It created an additional link between the store and the customer. "We wanted to bond our customers to us," he said. "We wanted to be able to solicit them for future business and obtain vertical control of a customer's purchasing experience."

By offering direct financing to its customers, R.C. Willey discovered another hidden advantage stemming from a complicated IRS income tax provision that applied to retailers who collected payment on an installment basis. Generally, a retailer who makes a $100 profit on a piece of merchandise is required to pay roughly $30 in income taxes at the time the purchase is made, whether that sale is paid for in cash or on credit. But by taking advantage of the tax provision for the installment basis for reporting income, R.C. Willey wasn't paying the $30 in taxes until the customer completed his installment payments. During the interim, the store incurred no interest or penalty fees from the IRS.

"It was like getting a loan without paying interest or collateral," Bill said. "By financing the sales ourselves, we were able to defer the income tax payments until we actually collected the sale. And the larger our portfolio got, the more taxes we could delay."

Eventually, R.C. Willey's portfolio reached a point where it had more than $6 million in deferred taxes. "It was like finding $6 million," Bill said. "Uncle Sam let us keep the money with no interest or collateral. The situation gave us $6 million that our competitors didn't have and provided the funds to finance our expansion and growth."

When the government eventually changed the law on deferred tax payments, it gave R.C. Willey four years to pay back the $6 million in deferred taxes.

The store got another windfall after Jimmy Carter was elected president and the prime interest rate skyrocketed to twenty-one percent. Under those conditions, even banks and credit cards weren't lending money to retail furniture and appliance stores. It was just too expensive. As a result, almost no retailers could afford to sell merchandise on credit. Customers who couldn't afford to pay cash were simply out of luck.

At that time, R.C. Willey was charging eighteen percent interest to its customers. With the prime rate at twenty-one percent, that meant the store was taking a three percent loss every time it sold merchandise on credit. "Most MBAs would have looked at our situation," Bill pointed out, "and said this makes no sense. How can you finance at eighteen percent when the prime is twenty-one? You're paying prime rate for your money."

But that time turned out to be one of the biggest growth periods in the company's history. With consumers having almost no place else to buy merchandise on credit, they flocked to R.C. Willey. The store didn't feel the hit it was taking on financing because its sales volume was sky high. And the high volume pushed down the cost of operations. "The reason we sold so much is that we were financing our own customer accounts," Bill explained. "Most other stores couldn't sell unless the customer paid cash. We gained considerable market share during this time."

By the mid-1980s, R.C. Willey was taking in more than $7 million in annual profits through self-financing. And by the early 1990s, R.C. Willey's credit card profits surpassed $18 million annually. "Everyone agreed that being a bank was a profitable venture," Bill said. "We were just adding one more financial benefit to our operation."

6. Hire the right personnel.

A big part of the success of R.C. Willey's credit operation had to do with who was overseeing it. "Granting credit can be risky," Bill said. "I wanted someone running the operation who could understand and accurately analyze an applicant's credit history. In other words, someone who was good at establishing a sound credit policy."

Bill decided to aim high. His top choice to oversee the store's credit department was Michael Boswell, a banker specializing in risk analysis for Key Bank in Salt Lake City. Boswell had handled the R.C. Willey accounts for a number of years so Bill knew him personally and had been very impressed with his knowledge and expertise.

But convincing Boswell to leave Key Bank for R.C. Willey would not be easy. Before even approaching Boswell, Bill contacted the president of Key Bank and requested permission. R.C. Willey enjoyed a great relationship with the bank and it was important to protect that. The president appreciated Bill's approach and cleared the way for R.C. Willey to speak with Boswell.

Bill personally interviewed Boswell, a move that confirmed his inclination to offer him the position as the company's director of credit. Boswell accepted. Under his leadership, R.C. Willey established a very lucrative finance operation. Equally important, the store developed a reputation for being careful and prudent in its lending practices with customers. "We never wanted to sell a product that a customer couldn't afford," Bill said. "If a customer is overextended with credit, he has a miserable experience when struggling to pay for something. It puts a hardship on him. So we were very careful in extending credit."

Finding the right personnel often means looking in unlikely places and never being afraid of a job candidate, even when it appears that a candidate is unlikely to accept. Just as R.C. Willey was entering its growth phase in the 1970s, Bill felt it was time to hire a full-time secretary. For years he had relied on a pool of part-time secretaries, each of whom assisted a number of management staff. He needed someone dedicated exclusively to answering his calls, handling his correspondence, and helping him keep his calendar.

The kind of person he had in mind was a lot like a legal secretary he had observed in the law firm that handled R.C. Willey's legal work. Marcia Garner impressed Bill every time he was in his lawyer's office. Besides demonstrating efficiency, professionalism, and an attractive appearance, Garner displayed an impressive knowledge of legal and business issues. However, he figured someone of her talent and ability might not be interested in a secretarial position for a retail furniture executive.

One day Bill was meeting with his lawyer and mentioned to him that he was looking for a full-time assistant. He was shocked when his lawyer suggested that Bill pursue Garner who had recently retired from the law firm.

"Oh, I'd love to have someone like her," Bill said.

"She was so efficient that we couldn't keep her busy," Bill's lawyer told him. "She was bored and decided to retire."

Garner's husband had been a very successful businessman in his own right, removing the necessity of her staying in the workforce.

"Well," Bill said, "do you think she'd be interested in working for us?"

Bill's lawyer wasn't sure. But he was confident Bill would have no regrets if he offered Garner the position.

There were all kinds of reasons not to bother contacting Garner. Money wouldn't motivate her; she didn't need an income. She didn't live close to the Syracuse store, resulting in a longer commute than most of the store's employees. Plus, Bill didn't even have an office for her; Garner would have to share space with other secretaries. Nonetheless, he called her and made the most positive, appealing offer he could muster.

To Bill's delight, Garner agreed to come out of retirement and work for him. She ended up being Bill's right hand for seventeen years. "During our growth years, she was vital," Bill said. "I would have been totally overwhelmed without her. I could count on her to make decisions that I'd never have to review. She could almost anticipate what I needed and wanted to do."

Eventually, Garner became the supervisor over all corporate purchasing secretaries. "I don't know how I impressed her enough to have her come to work for us in the beginning," Bill said. "She is one of the great employees who helped make our company so successful."

7. Treat employees like family.

As R.C. Willey transitioned from a small family operation with one or two employees to a retail chain with hundreds of employees, Bill and Sheldon wanted to maintain a corporate climate that still felt like family. They started referring to employees as associates and they treated them the way they preferred to be treated. They also made a point to show their appreciation regularly.

For example, after Bill acquired a potato farm in Idaho, he brought every R.C. Willey employee a fifty-pound bag of Idaho potatoes every year at harvest time. "It doesn't take a lot to do things like that," Bill said. "But it means a lot."

The company also instituted a generous profit-sharing plan. R.C. Willey offered to contribute the maximum allowable percentage of an individual's salary into an account each year. This enabled employees to obtain annual, tax-free contributions from the company. It took six years for an employee's rights to fully vest. For those who remained with the company for twenty to thirty years, the profit-sharing plan produced a substantial nest egg that had accumulated tax-free.

"That's one of the secrets to our success," Bill said. "Our employees buy into the mission of our company. If they feel as though they own a part of the company, they will do a great job. They will be cautious. They will look at expenses. And they will try to maximize profits."

The profit-sharing plan had another benefit: employees told other people about the greatness of the company and that, in turn, created more customers and produced a steady flow of quality applicants for employment at the stores.

8. Build a business to keep, not to sell.

Even after R.C. Willey started to enjoy tremendous financial success, Bill constantly was on the hunt for ways to improve the company. Not having a formal education in business, he set aside one or two weeks a year to attend business seminars at the leading business schools in America. He made a point to attend seminars that offered knowledge and information on how to better manage, market, and grow a retail company. One of his favorites was the biannual senior management retail seminar at Harvard Business School. Besides analyzing many successful companies, Bill and his seminar colleagues examined companies that had failed due to poor management. "As we see today," Bill said, "some executives feel they are entitled to outrageous salaries and lots of perks and that the business is obligated to support a lavish lifestyle without regard for the shareholders' interest in the future of the company."

One seminar topic that particularly interested Bill had to do with motives for starting a company. A popular theme that emerged in these seminars was the concept of starting a business for the purpose of growing it, maximizing its profits, and then selling it in order to start another business. That's not necessarily a bad approach, but Bill had built R.C. Willey into a successful company by doing just the opposite. He could have taken the profits out of the business; instead, he opted for a modest salary, enabling the store to accumulate more savings in reserve. He also chose not to draw himself bonuses or dividends at the end of each year. Rather, he and Sheldon kept putting most of the company's profits back into the business.

To Bill, the idea of building a company to see how much he could personally squeeze out of it didn't make a lot of sense. "Anyone who builds a business with a strong foundation will create a situation where the company's future is always greater than its past," Bill said. "And in most cases it doesn't make sense to sell a business that has a more promising future."

CHAPTER ELEVEN

■ ■ ■

IF YOU BUILD IT,
THEY WILL COME

Around the time that Bill decided to build the Murray store, he attended a retail conference in Chicago. While there, he visited a Polk Bros. Inc. store, founded by legendary salesman Sol Polk in 1935. Sol and his five siblings sold appliances and electronics, growing the business into a chain of seventeen stores throughout Chicago. Many of his stores were across from each other on one street called Polk City. During the 1960s Polk Bros. was the largest retail appliance business in the United States. Sol later added furniture to the stores, and he was eventually named president of the North American Retail Dealers Association.

Bill had heard so much about Sol and his company that he wanted to see one of the stores for himself. He came away both impressed and discouraged. The displays and overall product presentation at Polk Bros. were so outstanding that it made the R.C. Willey store look like it needed a face-lift. When Bill returned to Utah, he immediately set out to change the atmosphere and the appearance on the sales floor. The furniture, he decided, needed to be arranged to create the impression of actual rooms in a home. In other words, living room furniture should be set up to look like a living room; bedroom furniture should be set up to look like a bedroom.

Eventually, R.C. Willey hired an interior designer and gave him the full-time task of decorating the stores. Displays were accented with lamps, area rugs, pictures, and other accessories that made the showroom look and feel like the interior of a beautiful home. The new approach made the R.C. Willey stores look like a series of rooms, which gave the showroom an inviting, comfortable, and attractive feel. And to maintain a fresh look, the designer routinely changed the furniture arrangements and design backdrops.

Ten years after visiting Polk Bros., Bill was back in Chicago with Sheldon. He insisted that Sheldon see for himself the tremendous presentation at Polk City. This time, however, Bill was not impressed. The Chicago store looked exactly the way it had a decade earlier. The displays had not been updated. The feel was the same. Even the carpet was the same. The store felt stale and stagnant.

Bill came away persuaded that the R.C. Willey stores had become far more attractive than the Polk Bros. stores. The experience also convinced him that change is an essential ingredient for success in the retail industry. Companies that don't adapt don't last. Polk Bros. eventually went out of business, overcome by a recession and competition from newcomers such as Circuit City and Best Buy.

Polk Bros. was hardly the first major furniture or appliance retailer to go out of business. When Bill first got into the appliance business, companies such as Magnavox and Motorola were giants in the television industry. Similarly, furniture retailers such as Levitz and wholesalers such as Lane seemed invincible. But eventually, all of these companies and many others went out of business or were forced to drastically retool their business model.

Despite seeing scores of furniture stores come and go in Utah, Bill managed to keep R.C. Willey profitable year after year by paying attention to a statement that an old banker told him shortly after Bill had taken over the store: *There are three things you can count on—death, taxes, and change.*

"He was right about change," Bill said. "The world changes. Many of the furniture companies that have gone out of business have done so because they failed to change."

A company's need to change is driven by the fact that customers' needs and expectations change. The competition changes too. When Bill first took over R.C. Willey, his competition was one or two furniture and appliance stores. Later, department stores arrived on the scene. Then catalogs came along. Eventually, stores such as Wal-Mart, Costco, Sam's Club, Home Depot, and Lowe's began offering household items. Ultimately, online shopping enabled customers to acquire virtually every kind of furniture item and appliance without leaving the home. These innovations forced many of R.C. Willey's competitors out of business.

To keep its business vibrant, R.C. Willey made sure to always update what it offered customers in terms of merchandise. Bill personally visited trade shows around the world, searching for the newest products that would satisfy customers' desires. For instance, when exercise bikes became the rage, R.C. Willey didn't hesitate to stock its stores with them, even though the store hadn't previously carried exercise equipment in its inventory. The result was that the company sold more than 10,000 exercise bikes in one year.

At the same time, the store constantly changed its interior appearance. By hiring a highly accomplished interior decorator and giving him authority and encouragement to keep the sales floors fresh and inviting, R.C. Willey sent a signal that appearance and atmosphere were a top priority. As a result, the company didn't fall into the trap that many furniture stores encounter, becoming beholden to a certain appearance and model. "Change can come gradually and sneak up on you," Bill said. "Many of our competitors kept doing the same thing, expecting the same results while the world was changing around them."

Eager to stay one step ahead of his competitors in the Utah market, Bill continued to focus on growth. In 1984, R.C. Willey Home Furnishings surpassed $51 million in annual sales. A year later the company opened its third store—this one in West Valley, another Salt Lake City suburb not far from the Murray store.

Bill hoped to build more stores. But first R.C. Willey

had to change the way it delivered merchandise to its stores and to its customers through home delivery. The company's transportation infrastructure simply wasn't capable of handling any more business.

In the late 1980s, R.C. Willey approached the South Salt Lake City mayor and proposed building a massive distribution center with a retail store and corporate offices inside the city limits if the city would help identify a large enough tract of land at a reasonable price. The city came back with a thirteen-acre block in a blighted neighborhood right off Interstate 15. Thirteen small businesses occupied the land. Not all of them wanted to relocate; it was up to R.C. Willey to buy them out and in one case put up the money to physically move one business to another part of the city.

Some executives at R.C. Willey were skeptical; they were convinced a retail store would never succeed in the part of town being contemplated. They argued that shoppers wouldn't travel to a blighted area to shop for home furnishings. Bill saw it differently. He maintained that if the store and the grounds around it were constructed properly, R.C. Willey had the potential to revitalize the neighborhood. And by erecting a gigantic distribution center alongside the interstate, they'd have the biggest, permanent billboard in the city.

By 1989, R.C. Willey had secured all thirteen acres and broken ground on a 280,000-square-foot distribution center. The center would be divided into 180,000 square feet of warehouse, 30,000 square feet of corporate offices, and

70,000 square feet of furniture display. It was one of the largest retail furniture facilities of its kind in the United States. When the doors opened in 1990, R.C. Willey had instant exposure that dwarfed every other furniture retailer in the city. That year, gross sales surpassed $85 million.

With three stores, a warehouse, and a corporate headquarters within ten miles of each other, R.C. Willey emerged as the dominant furniture and appliance retailer in the greater Salt Lake City area. With so much exposure, Bill began receiving all sorts of invitations to join corporate boards and charitable organizations. But he politely declined most of the invitations in order to focus on his business.

A Call from the Church
March 1991

Located in the center of North Carolina, the city of High Point is known as "The Furniture Capital of the World," thanks to its abundance of furniture manufacturers and textile mills. Semiannually, the city hosts the High Point Market, a furniture exhibition that attracts more than 100,000 sellers and buyers from around the world. When Sheldon became the sales director and president of R.C. Willey in 1971, he began attending the exhibition with Bill. They had been going back to North Carolina together for twenty years.

Just before leaving for the High Point Market in 1991, Sheldon was summoned to a meeting with an apostle of The Church of Jesus Christ of Latter-day Saints at the Church headquarters in Salt Lake City. In addition to his corporate responsibilities at R.C. Willey, Sheldon had spent the previous nine and half years as an ecclesiastical leader—known as a stake president—responsible for the spiritual and temporal welfare of 5,800 Mormons in the town of Syracuse. He'd already been informed that the Church would be releasing him from his duties as a stake president. He figured the Church official wanted to meet with him to discuss his departure.

But in the meeting, Sheldon was asked whether he'd be willing to serve in a full-time capacity for the Church. No specific position was discussed. The purpose of the interview was merely to inquire whether Sheldon was in a position to take on added responsibility.

Sheldon indicated that the timing wasn't particularly good for him, but if the Church asked him to serve, he'd honor that request. He left the meeting feeling confident that no assignment would be issued.

But while in High Point with Bill, Sheldon received a phone call from his wife. "You got a call from the Church today," she told him. "They want you to come in for an interview when you get back."

The request had come from the office of President Thomas S. Monson, First Counselor in the First Presidency of the Church.

Sheldon had trouble focusing on furniture—or anything else—for the rest of the trip. He was completely unprepared for what transpired when he arrived at President Monson's office—a calling was extended to serve as the president of the Church's proselytizing mission in New York City. It was a full-time assignment that would require Sheldon to move his family across the country and supervise more than 150 young men and women assigned to missions in New York. "You'll have to be ready to go by July first," President Monson told him. "Can you do that?"

Bill wasn't surprised when his brother reported the news. "I knew that sooner or later the Church was going to call you," Bill told him.

Besides being company president over sales, Sheldon was in charge of buying all of the company's upholstered goods. "We're going to have to get someone to replace you," Bill said.

Sheldon helped find a successor. Then, two months later, he packed up his office, said good-bye to his brother, and left for New York City on a three-year leave of absence from the company. For the first time since 1956, Bill was without his younger brother in the business.

Sheldon had barely been gone a few weeks when Bill picked up the morning paper and discovered a gigantic advertisement from his closest competitor in Utah—Granite Furniture. In the ad, Granite announced it was building its fourth superstore—this one in Layton, just miles from the R.C. Willey store in Syracuse. Once that occurred, many customers would have to pass by Granite Furniture to get to the R.C. Willey store.

"For 81 years Utah has watched furniture stores start up and grow and then suddenly disappear," the ad said, before listing the names of forty Utah retail stores and wholesale distributors that had gone out of business. "Granite Furniture Company is as solid as the rock we were named after. We've always given the best values for the money."

Bill saved the advertisement.

Over the next three years, R.C. Willey experienced its biggest growth in the company's history. The massive distribution center had a lot to do with the success. One reason that some questioned the wisdom of building such a huge facility was that it came on the heels of a nationwide economic slowdown. On the surface, it didn't seem like a good time to be building a superstore and a gigantic warehouse. But Utah's economy had fared better than the national average, and in 1990, business in Utah took off, particularly for the retail furniture business. Thanks to the warehouse, R.C. Willey was in a position to provide for the consumers.

"That's why we had such great growth in those years—we had an infrastructure where we could receive and deliver merchandise," Bill said. "We had space to store a big inventory. We could provide next-day deliveries. And we had an efficient warehouse."

On the other hand, Granite Furniture, R.C. Willey's primary competitor in the Salt Lake City market, had not done anything to increase its warehousing capability. It had only added new superstores. In the end, Granite ended up liquidating and closing its doors, leaving R.C. Willey as the largest furniture company in Utah.

R.C. Willey realized that it is important to generate sales, but it is equally important to maintain a warehousing infrastructure to support those sales. "It takes time to assimilate growth," Bill said. "If you grow too fast, the infra-structure and systems of a company aren't able to handle it. Those must grow at the same level that sales grow. Otherwise, a company becomes inefficient in the delivery of its product. The result is higher costs and decreased cus-tomer satisfaction."

CHAPTER TWELVE

■ ■ ■

"A JEWEL OF A COMPANY"

January 1995
San Francisco, California

Bill had been going to the San Francisco Furniture Market every year since the early sixties to check out product samples from furniture manufacturers. He always looked forward to previewing the newest lines and determining which ones would be successful in his stores. But this time around, he had something else on his mind: $200 million. That's how much an investment bank had recently offered for R.C. Willey Home Furnishings.

Previously, two national furniture store chains had also made inquiries about acquiring R.C. Willey. Heilig-Meyers Co., the country's largest publicly traded home furnishing retailer approached Bill in 1994, right after the company hit the $1 billion mark in annual sales revenues. But Bill felt the company's management style wasn't a good fit for R.C.

Willey. He also turned down Montgomery Ward after visiting one of its large stores in the Phoenix area and coming away unimpressed.

Bill was under no pressure to sell and hadn't solicited any offers, but an active mergers and acquisitions climate on Wall Street had put some focus on R.C. Willey's growth, outstanding profit margins, and low debt ratios. It had taken Bill and Sheldon forty years, but through persistence and adherence to time-tested principles, they had taken the company from $250,000 in sales per year to $250 million by 1994. Better still, the business had no mortgages and only borrowed money to finance its accounts receivable.

If Bill accepted the investment bank's $200 million offer, R.C. Willey's financial condition would change overnight. The bank was offering to put up $100 million in cash, while borrowing the rest of the purchase price by using R.C. Willey's assets as collateral. This arrangement insured that Bill and Sheldon would walk away with all of their money. But the company would then be saddled with $100 million in debt, a scenario that went against what Bill had spent forty years avoiding. He told the investment bank no thanks.

But turning sixty-three years old had him thinking hard about the past and the future. He remembered how an unexpected illness had forced his father-in-law to give up the business. Bill didn't want to end up in a similar situation. Rather, he wanted to see the business continue for decades to come. His biggest concern was finding the right person to hand the baton to. Sheldon was back from his three-year duty as mission president in New York and had resumed his duties at the company, but he was already beginning to transition out of the company. Bill suspected it was only a matter of time before his brother would be asked to fill another Church assignment, one that would likely bring a permanent end to his business career.

Bill figured it was time he started preparing for a transition, too. Yet he couldn't come to grips with selling a business that he had spent his entire adult life building.

While in San Francisco, Bill ran into his longtime friend Irv Blumkin, the CEO of Nebraska Furniture Mart, the largest furniture store in North America. Blumkin listened as Bill explained his predicament. It was a scenario familiar to Blumkin because back in 1983, his family had faced a similar situation. It controlled the biggest retail furniture store in Nebraska and one of the most profitable home furnishing businesses in the country. That year, the family had decided to sell eighty percent of its company to Warren Buffett and Berkshire Hathaway Inc. for $60 million.

Bill asked how things had turned out.

Blumkin said the family could not be happier. The deal was reached over a handshake, and Buffett had honored every promise. It was difficult, Blumkin insisted, to imagine a better business partner. Best of all, the family hadn't had to surrender the family business. The ownership changed, but the family continued to run the company.

"Irv," Bill asked, "do you think Warren would be interested in buying our company?"

Blumkin couldn't see why not. R.C. Willey was considered one of the best retail furniture companies in the industry.

He offered to put Bill in touch with Buffett if Bill decided he wanted to explore the possibility of selling to Berkshire Hathaway.

Bill couldn't stop thinking about his conversation with Blumkin. After reading up on Buffett, his company, and his leadership style, Bill talked with Sheldon, who immediately agreed that if they were to sell, selling to Buffett would be a best-case scenario.

A few days later Bill and Blumkin were together again, this time at an industry function in Pebble Beach, California. Bill wanted to take Blumkin up on his offer to contact Buffett.

Blumkin said he was having dinner with Buffett in the coming week and would talk to him about R.C. Willey.

Mid-February

It was late in the afternoon and most of the office staff at R.C. Willey's corporate office had gone home for the day. Bill was working late as usual when a call came through on his private line. Irv Blumkin had some good news.

"I talked to Warren," he said. "He's really interested in talking to you about your company, and he's going to call you."

A few minutes after hanging up with Blumkin, Bill received another call.

"This is Warren Buffett, Bill. I just talked to Irv, and I understand you have an interest in selling your company."

"Have you got a few minutes? By the way, I'm awfully

flattered that you'd call," Bill said, hardly able to believe that he was talking to Warren Buffett.

"I've got all the time in the world," Buffett said.

At the outset, Bill wanted Buffett to know why he was interested in selling. "I want to be sure the company continues beyond my lifetime," Bill explained. "Second, if anything were to happen to me or my wife the business would have to be sold at a fire-sale price to pay the estate tax."

Succession, Buffett acknowledged, is a common challenge. But Buffett didn't typically buy companies that were about to undergo a change in management; he preferred companies with well-established leadership. He asked Bill how long he planned on remaining the CEO.

"For as long as I can be productive and make a contribution," Bill said.

Buffett said he couldn't buy the business if Bill didn't remain at the helm.

"I can promise you at least seven years," Bill said. "And then we can find somebody who will continue to run it."

Buffett accepted that and asked Bill how much he wanted for the company.

"Just a fair price," Bill responded, adding that he'd like an acquisition similar to the one that the Blumkin family had when it sold its company to Buffett and was able to retain twenty percent of the company. "We want whoever buys it to be just as happy ten years from now as they are the day they buy the company."

That sounded reasonable to Buffett. "If you are interested in selling," he told Bill, "I would love to look at it."

"What would you like me to do?" Bill asked.

"I already know a lot about the company," Buffett said. "Just send me the previous two or three years' worth of financial statements from the company, along with some history."

Within twenty-four hours of talking to Buffett, Bill had compiled all the requested documents and mailed them overnight to the Berkshire Hathaway office in Omaha. Buffett liked what he saw. The company had steadily enjoyed an average of seventeen percent growth in sales and profit each year. It had just opened its sixth store in Utah, and the company was grossing close to $260 million a year. R.C. Willey was far and away the top-selling furniture chain in the state of Utah. It accounted for more than fifty percent of the furniture sold in Utah, blowing away the closest competitor. The store also led the state in consumer electronics sales, controlling almost thirty-five percent of the market share. Computer sales alone topped $20 million annually. R.C. Willey also had 133,000 active revolving credit accounts—customers who were making monthly principal and interest payments to the store for merchandise purchased on store-issued credit cards.

But one aspect of the business really jumped out: R.C. Willey had no debt. All its land and buildings were paid for, a result of Bill's pay-as-you-go philosophy from when he first took over the company.

Four days after receiving Bill's package, Buffett sent him a confidential letter, saying R.C. Willey was "a jewel of a company" and promising to have him a purchase price within three days.

Several days later, a second letter arrived from Buffett, who said he had mixed emotions about whether a possible transaction should be for all or part of the business. Stressing his preference for simplicity and pointing out that it would be cleaner for Berkshire Hathaway to acquire a hundred percent of R.C. Willey, Buffett nonetheless left the door open to purchasing a percentage of the company, albeit not less than eighty percent. "All in all," he wrote, "I would say that if you and your brother had a significant preference for retaining a piece of the business, that would be fine with me, but if it was not a matter of great importance one way or the other, I would prefer a transaction for 100%."

Buffett also promised a seamless transition:

> The day after the transaction, the company would be run just as before, and the same would be true five or ten years later. R.C. Willey would retain its identity as a local institution, and the world would never think about the fact that Berkshire Hathaway owned it. In the case of See's Candy, for example, which we bought in 1972, I believe that 99% of its customers think of it as a strictly California institution. You would be the CEO and you would never need to make a trip to Omaha. . . .
>
> We could make a transaction for either cash or stock. It would seem to me, however, that if you wished to do a cash transaction—which would be

taxable—it would be a good idea to wait and see what Congress does with the capital gains tax. It is overwhelmingly likely that your business will grow in value over time, so there is no reason to hurry a transaction that would be taxable when a lowering of tax rates is possible. If you wish to have a stock transaction, of course that would be non-taxable. We will arrange to have your Berkshire stock registered and fully marketable. . . .

On a 100% basis, Berkshire could pay $170 million in either cash or stock.

Buffett closed his letter by leaving his personal phone number and inviting Bill to call him if the offer appealed to him.

Bill recognized that Buffett's proposed purchase price was $20 million to $30 million below the other offers he had received. But there was so much more to Buffett's offer that fit what Bill and Sheldon were looking for: they'd get to continue running the business, customers wouldn't notice a change in ownership, and Buffett was known for his impeccable integrity. If Bill and Sheldon were going to sell R.C. Willey, it was going to be to Warren Buffett.

First, Bill called Irv Blumkin and thanked him.

"My advice to you," Blumkin told Bill, "is that no matter what you do, take stock. Had we taken stock instead of cash—and held it—it would have been worth over a billion dollars today."

Next, Bill called a trusted personal friend who was an

investment banker at Citigroup's Salt Lake City office. The banker had evaluated many companies and was personally familiar with R.C. Willey's financial picture due to the store's business relationship with Citigroup. At Bill's request, he agreed to come to the R.C. Willey headquarters for a confidential conversation.

"Is this a fair offer?" Bill asked his friend, pushing Buffett's letter across the desk.

The banker read it over. "It's a fair offer," he said. "But it's on the low side."

Bill explained that he had already turned down offers from a couple of investment banks and competitors who had each offered over $20 million more. But he really wanted to sell to Buffett.

"Why don't you negotiate with Warren?" the banker suggested.

"If Warren buys the company I'm going to be working with him and for him," Bill explained. "I'm not too comfortable in negotiating with him."

Bill also figured $170 million was a lot of money. It was more important to find an owner that would take care of the employees and the customers, and there was no doubt Buffett would do both.

After talking with the investment banker, Bill sat down with Sheldon and they reviewed everything. Together, they agreed that they should proceed. Bill called Buffett.

"Warren, I got your offer," he said. "I think it's very fair."

Buffett was pleased.

"We'd very much like you to come out and take a look at our operation," Bill said.

"I don't need to come and look at it," Buffett said. "You have a wonderful reputation. I know that if you say the assets are there, then they are there, plus some."

After a long conversation, Bill said, "Warren, there's no way I could sell this company to you without you first seeing what you are buying. It just wouldn't be fair."

After reviewing his calendar, Buffett said he was headed to Palm Springs to play golf with Bill Gates. He said he'd stop in Salt Lake City on the way.

CHAPTER THIRTEEN

∎ ∎ ∎

A COKE AND A HAMBURGER

After R.C. Willey had opened multiple stores and Bill became the company's CEO, he made a habit of dedicating his Saturdays to visiting his stores. It was a great way to stay in touch with the needs of his employees and customers. While at a store, he inspected everything, from the warehouse to the furniture store display arrangements. He'd even pick up litter and tidy up the restrooms.

Bill never called ahead to say he was coming, preferring the element of surprise. But once he got to the first store on his itinerary for the day, the other stores would get a call, warning them: "Bill's on his way." That gave other store managers time to get the place looking great before he arrived.

Bill decided not to give his store managers advance

warning that Buffett would be in town to inspect the stores. He preferred that Buffett see things under everyday conditions. There was another more important reason to keep Buffett's visit hush-hush. No one except Bill and Sheldon and a couple of senior executives had any idea that the company might be sold. If word got out prematurely, unnecessary anxiety could sweep through the employee ranks, generating all sorts of unfounded fears about how a change in ownership might adversely affect jobs and stability.

Instead, Bill planned to simply show up with Buffett, much the same way he did when any number of other high-powered business executives showed up to tour his stores. But Bill did take steps to ensure that he and Sheldon do everything possible to make Buffett's visit a pleasant one. He even called Buffett's assistant Debbie Bosanek to find out what kind of food he preferred.

"Just get him a hamburger and a Coke," Bosanek told Bill. "That's all he wants."

One of the reasons Bill and Sheldon wanted Buffett to visit their stores was to see firsthand if he was as pleasant and down-to-earth as he had been described by the Blumkins. They wanted to make absolutely certain that they were completely comfortable with the man who would be assuming ownership of their company. When Buffett's secretary told Bill to simply buy Buffett a hamburger, Bill knew one thing—there was nothing pretentious about the guy.

Nonetheless, Bill was a bit nervous as Buffett emerged from his private jet at the airport in Salt Lake City, wearing a navy blue suit, maroon tie, and a white shirt.

"Hi, Bill," Buffett said, smiling as he extended his hand.

"Well, hello, Warren," Bill said before introducing him to Sheldon and the others who were on hand from the company: Bill's sons David and Steve, Sheldon's son-in-law Scott Hymas, and the company's CFO, Richard Turnbow.

Although his contact with Buffett had been limited to a few phone calls, Bill already felt as though he knew him. The group piled into Scott Hymas's van and headed for the main store in Salt Lake City, giving Buffett a chance to see the distribution center and the corporate headquarters, along with some retail space. Buffett liked what he saw—the place was clean, and bustling with customers.

As the group toured the other stores around Salt Lake City, Bill stressed the company's desire to build even more stores.

"Now we're closed on Sundays," Bill informed Buffett. "If we ever expand, we'd want to remain closed on Sundays."

In most markets, Sunday is the top day for in-store sales. But Buffett didn't object to R.C. Willey's policy. He knew Bill and Sheldon were Mormons and that their faith had a lot to do with their closed-on-Sundays policy. "Well," Buffett said, "if you can produce these kinds of sales and profit numbers, we'll be glad to support you in being closed on Sundays."

On the way to the Syracuse store, Bill brought up the subject of Berkshire Hathaway's stock value. He explained that many years earlier he had considered purchasing some Berkshire stock when it was valued at $2,500 per share. By the time he got around to telling his broker to make the purchase, however, the stock had jumped to $5,000 and Bill hesitated. A few years later he again approached his broker and told him to make the acquisition, but by then the stock had risen to $7,500 per share. Again, Bill hesitated. Just before Buffett touched down in Salt Lake City, Bill checked the Berkshire stock and it was selling for $22,000 per share. But a couple weeks earlier the price was down.

"Warren, valuing common stock is a little confusing to me," Bill said, hoping Buffett could explain something to him. When it came to R.C. Willey, Bill could track its value on a day-to-day basis. Every month the company's net worth increased about $2 million. But Bill had been tracking the Berkshire Hathaway stock for a number of years—it often fluctuated, making it difficult to determine the true value of the stock. If Bill agreed to accept Berkshire stock in exchange for selling R.C. Willey, he wondered what the value of the stock would be at the time of the sale.

"I can understand your concern," Buffett said. "But the stock is now at $22,000 a share. I'll tell you what I'll do. I'll lock it in at $22,000 if we do the deal."

Bill asked what would happen if the stock price increased.

"If it goes up," Buffett said, "that's to your benefit."

"What if the value goes down?" Bill asked.

"Then we'll talk about it," Buffett said.

Bill accepted that as being extremely fair.

After visiting most of the company's stores, Bill checked his watch. It was almost time to drive Buffett back to the airport.

"We've got to at least get you something to eat," Bill said.

"Let's just get us a hamburger," Buffett said.

Bill smiled.

"In a hurry I realized that this guy is real," he recalled. "He's exactly the kind of guy you want to be in business with or to go fishing or golfing with. He's just wonderful to be around, and he makes you feel important. Yet I could tell how intelligent he was by the way he answered my questions."

Before stopping by the Syracuse store, the group drove Buffett to Crown Burger, a drive-up, fast-food place on Main Street in nearby Layton. Buffett ordered his customary Coca-Cola and a hamburger. They all ate in the van while hustling over to the Syracuse store before heading back toward Salt Lake City. They had seen all the R.C. Willey stores except one.

"I've seen all I need to see," Buffett said, obviously impressed with the overall operation.

Before Buffett boarded his private plane, Bill pulled him aside.

"Well," Bill said, "what do you think?"

"You have a good business," Buffett said. "If you want to sell it, I'd like to buy it."

"You've got my vote," Bill said. "Let me talk it over with the family."

Bill's son David—a lawyer specializing in taxation—thought it made sense to try to pull some tax-free cash out of the sale to Buffett, rather than going with an all-stock transaction. Typically, cash derived from a sale they obtained for the company would be subject to income tax; stock transactions were not subject to taxation until the stock was sold. But Bill's son was convinced there was a way to draw some cash from the sale of the company without being subjected to income taxes. Bill called Buffett.

"I've talked to the family and we're all in favor of selling to you," he said. "However, it needs to be a tax-free transaction for us to sell the company."

A few years earlier, R.C. Willey had changed from a C Corp to an S Corp. As a result, it had accumulated some earnings, and the income taxes on those earnings had already been paid. There were a number of technicalities that would enable them to recover those earnings under the tax code. Bill and his family just needed a little more time to figure it out. Buffett agreed to hold his offer price of $170 million for the company, entitling Bill to receive Berkshire stock valued at $22,000 per share.

For the next couple of weeks, Bill and David struggled with the tax question. Each week Buffett called to see if they'd come to a resolution. But they hadn't found a way to do it. Finally, Buffett made a suggestion.

"Bill, I can't guarantee you won't pay taxes," he said. "But if it will help, I'll add another $5 million to the pot."

"Warren, you don't have to do that," Bill said.

"I'd like to," he said.

Bill didn't have to think twice. In the three-week period since they'd started looking into the tax question, the Berkshire Hathaway stock had risen from $22,000 a share to $24,000 a share. Yet Buffett was still offering to buy R.C. Willey with Berkshire stock valued at $22,000. Now, on top of that, he was offering an additional $5 million.

He didn't bother calling his son for advice. "Warren, if you do that, you've got a deal right now. It's all stock."

A month later Berkshire Hathaway sent papers to Bill and other shareholders for their signatures prior to closing the sale. When Bill and his chief financial officer reviewed the papers, they discovered that Berkshire had mistakenly issued Bill and his family four additional shares of Berkshire stock. The oversight added an additional $100,000 to the sale price.

Bill immediately picked up the phone and notified Marc Hamburg, Berkshire's vice president and treasurer. "You made a miscalculation," he told Hamburg. "There are four extra shares, approximately $100,000 in our favor."

"I'll talk to Warren about it and get back to you in the morning."

Buffett appreciated that Bill had brought the error to his attention. He had Hamburg call Bill back.

"Don't worry about it," Hamburg told Bill. "Warren wants you to have the extra shares."

■ ■ ■

CHAPTER FOURTEEN

A DEAL YOU CAN'T REFUSE

On May 29, 1995, Berkshire Hathaway officially acquired R.C. Willey for $175 million in stock. The irony wasn't lost on Bill. Rufus Call Willey got into the appliance business by working as a lineman for Utah Power & Light. He was able to remain in business by selling the power company's products and other merchandise that ran off electricity. Eventually, Utah Power & Light was acquired by Pacific Power, which Warren Buffett later acquired. Now Buffett owned both the power company and the appliance and furniture company that held such a prominent place in Bill's family history.

Bill could not get over the fact that he now worked for Warren Buffett, the man who financial experts from around the world looked to for direction and advice. Bill figured he'd learn a tremendous amount from Buffett while his business continued to grow.

One of the first things he discovered was that Buffett had a wonderful sense of humor and a diplomatic way of establishing boundaries. The first time Buffett visited Salt Lake City after buying R.C. Willey, Bill picked him up at the airport. Beforehand, Bill's stockbroker had shared a rumor that Buffett was buying McDonald's stock. The stockbroker wanted Bill to find out if that was true.

"My broker said there's a rumor that you are buying some McDonald's stock," Bill said to Buffett during the car ride from the airport.

"Bill, do you think the sphinxes are quiet?" Buffett asked.

Bill hesitated, visualizing the statuesque Egyptian figures with the body of a lion and the head of a man. "Yes, I do," he said.

"Well, I'm quieter," Buffett said, smiling politely.

Bill got the message—it was not appropriate to ask Buffett about any publicly traded stocks. He simply doesn't talk about what he's buying or selling.

But when it came to future plans for R.C. Willey, Buffett did have something to say. Whenever Buffett purchased a company, he preferred to maintain the status quo in terms of management. In the case of R.C. Willey, that meant that Bill would continue to call the shots when it came to advertising, marketing, sales, labor issues, and overall operations. The only thing that Buffett insisted on was that any major capital expenditures would require his approval. This exception wasn't in writing, but Bill and Buffett had a clear understanding between them. As a result, if R.C. Willey wanted to construct a building or a new retail store, Buffett had to sign off on it.

Even before selling to Berkshire Hathaway, Bill had his mind set on taking his company outside Utah. He'd been gearing up for the move by improving the company's operations systems and by training management to handle a major expansion. He'd also been doing his homework and concluded that Las Vegas was the place to start. Market research identified the metro area around Las Vegas as the fastest growing area in the United States. Roughly 8,000 new residents were moving into Clark County each month. Henderson—a suburb of Las Vegas—was the fastest growing city in the United States.

Bill had even worked with a real estate firm and identified some potential properties for constructing a store in Henderson. The sites were relatively affordable, large enough to accommodate expansion, and easily accessible. It was time to bring the idea to Buffett. Bill called and explained that he wanted to take Buffett to Las Vegas to look at some potential properties for a future store.

Buffett mentioned to Bill that he'd soon be heading to Las Vegas on business. Bill offered to meet Buffett in Vegas and arrange for a helicopter pilot to fly them over the areas that Bill had been eyeing. Buffett agreed.

Las Vegas, Nevada

When Bill caught up with Buffett at the Mirage Hotel, the CEO of Nebraska Furniture Mart, Irv Blumkin, was with him. Buffett and Blumkin were traveling together. Bill introduced them to a realtor and the four of them hopped aboard a chartered helicopter. The pilot flew them over the suburbs of Henderson and Summerline. Thousands of brand-new homes blanketed the landscape beneath them.

"Warren," Bill said, "look at all these houses and rooftops."

Buffett nodded.

"A couple of years ago," Bill continued, "this was desert. These houses keep encroaching on the desert."

Buffett continued nodding.

"It is mind-boggling what's happening here," Bill said.

Buffett said nothing as he looked down on the new housing sprawl.

At the conclusion of the aerial tour, the helicopter touched down.

"Well, what do you think?" Bill asked.

"We're not going to go," Buffett said.

Bill couldn't believe it. His business plan was solid. He figured an R.C. Willey store in Henderson could easily rival the profitability of any of the company's stores in Utah. If anything, he felt they were a little late in breaking into the Las Vegas market; all of the new homes they had just flown over were already filled with new home furnishings and appliances. Nonetheless, Bill remained convinced that the ongoing housing boom promised enough business to make a successful store.

Bill could think of only one thing that would discourage Buffett. Before selling to Berkshire Hathaway, Bill and Sheldon stressed how important it was to them to maintain the company's long-standing, closed-on-Sunday policy. Buffett had accepted the idea, saying that as long as the stores continued to produce, Berkshire Hathaway would honor the policy. But at that time, Bill hadn't mentioned anything to Buffett about expanding outside Utah.

"Warren, is it the Sunday closing?"

"Yes," said Buffett, who respected Bill's religious convictions and preferred not to pressure him to abandon his beliefs. "We're not going to open on Sunday. But we're also not going to go into a market where we can't be successful. And I don't think we can be successful in Las Vegas and still be closed on Sunday."

Bill disagreed.

However, Buffett had done some homework of his own. "All three of your friends told me that as even as good of an operator as you are, they wouldn't go into Vegas and be closed on Sundays," Buffett said.

The friends Buffett had talked to were Irv Blumkin, along with the CEOs of Star Furniture and Jordan's Furniture—each of which were owned by Berkshire Hathaway. Buffett had asked the three CEOs the same question: "Would you go to Las Vegas and be closed on Sundays?"

They each said no.

Research by industry analysts also suggested that R.C.

Willey would have a tough time in Las Vegas unless it opened on Sundays. "Twenty-three percent of home furnishings sales are transacted on Sunday," one leading retail furniture analyst reported. "That's almost a quarter of all sales. That's a national figure. It might be thirty-five percent in Las Vegas because of the weird hours people work."

Bill didn't want to argue the point. He understood where Buffett was coming from. Buffett was used to shopping on Sundays at the Nebraska Furniture Mart store in Omaha, a store that had a parking lot capable of accommodating more than 1,600 cars. Every Sunday the parking lot was jammed. It didn't seem possible that a furniture store that stayed closed on Sundays could compete against stores that stayed open.

March 1996

When Sheldon Child received a telephone call from Thomas S. Monson's office at Church Headquarters in Salt Lake City, he suspected another assignment might be coming his way. He was right. The Church asked him to make a five-year, full-time commitment. For starters, Sheldon and his wife would be assigned to live and work in the Philippine Islands.

Right after accepting the assignment, Sheldon talked to Bill. This time, he explained, his obligations to the Church were going to be even greater than when he was asked to preside over the mission in New York.

"This is going to be five years," Sheldon said. "There's

no way I can remain involved in the company. I'll be in the Philippines full-time. This is the end of my career with the company."

Bill understood. He and Sheldon worked together to find and train a permanent replacement, and a couple of months later Bill warmly said good-bye to his brother.

Though cool to the idea of expanding outside Utah, Buffett nonetheless supported Bill's push for a new distribution center. The company was approaching $200 million a year in sales and had outgrown its warehouse. Bill had found 72 acres of land near the Salt Lake City airport. He called Buffett to discuss the acquisition.

Buffett had just returned from California, where he had been looking at real estate to expand another company owned by Berkshire—See's Candy Shops, Inc. The price of commercial land being considered by See's was around $500,000 per acre. The land Bill wanted R.C. Willey to acquire was available for $22,000 an acre.

Buffett was elated. In 1997, R.C. Willey constructed an 860,000 square-foot intermountain distribution center next to the airport, making it the largest distribution center of its kind in the United States. Overnight, the massive warehouse improved R.C. Willey's ability to keep all of the stores in Utah stocked with new merchandise.

Nonetheless, Bill remained discouraged about being unable to break into the Las Vegas market. Recognizing that Buffett wasn't going to budge, Bill turned his expansion sights to Boise, Idaho, another high-growth area. The demographics in Boise were a lot like Utah, both economically and socially.

In many ways, the city reminded Bill a lot of what Salt Lake City had been like twenty years earlier. Also, Boise was only 285 miles away from R.C. Willey's new distribution center, making it close enough for trucks to make deliveries.

Bill called Buffett and proposed building a new store in Boise.

"No, I don't think so," said Buffett, who said he was satisfied with the company's performance in Utah. "We're doing okay."

Not long after Buffett turned him down, Bill called him back. He was pretty sure the closed-on-Sunday policy was still the major hurdle.

"You know," Bill said, "there are probably a lot more Mormons in Idaho than in Las Vegas."

"I don't think so," Buffett said. "You have a higher percentage of Mormons in Las Vegas than in Boise, Idaho."

Buffett was right. In the year 2000, approximately 90,000 Mormons lived in the greater Las Vegas-Henderson area.

Regardless of the numbers, Bill had a dilemma. To him it was obvious that if the company were going to grow, it had to build outside Utah—R.C. Willey simply didn't have much more market share to gain in its home state. But Buffett wasn't going to approve construction outside Utah with the stores being closed on Sunday.

One Monday morning, Bill was in the shower, unable to stop thinking about Boise. *If I'm going to convince Buffett to go to Boise,* he figured, *I've got to do something totally out of the box, something really dramatic.*

Bill didn't exit the shower until he had come up with an idea. Later that morning, after arriving at the office, he telephoned Buffett in Omaha.

"I'd like to talk to you about Boise, Idaho," he began.

"Bill, we've already talked about Boise," he said curtly.

"Warren, I'm going to make you a proposition you can't refuse," Bill said.

Buffett agreed to listen.

"I will buy the land, and I will build the building, personally," Bill said. "And if we're not successful in six months, we'll walk. That guarantees that the company won't lose a dime."

Buffett had nothing to lose. Bill was offering to use his own money to finance the acquisition of land and the construction of a building. And if the store didn't succeed in six months, they'd simply close it and walk away.

"Okay," Buffett said. "If the store can't do $30 million the first year, we'll walk. If the store does $30 million, I'll lease it from you and pay you four percent of gross sales."

Bill thought that was fair. But he wasn't finished. "I'm going to add one more component to the deal," he told Buffett. "If we are really successful, I'll sell the store back at exactly what it cost me, including no interest."

"Okay," Buffett said, before hanging up.

Bill had the green light. He went next door to the weekly staff management meeting and made an announcement.

"We're going to build a store in Boise, Idaho," he said enthusiastically. "Warren just gave his approval."

The management team was surprised and energized.

"There is just one condition," Bill continued. "I agreed to personally buy the land and build the store. And if we're not successful after six months, we'll close it. So we have to do it right."

Bill's decision to use personal resources rather than company money got people's attention. It was a very unorthodox approach that placed all the risk squarely on Bill. But it wasn't the first time in the company's history that he'd taken risks.

"This is our opportunity to build out of state," he told his management team, eager to test the company's business model in other markets. "This is very important. We have a lot of talent and we need to keep expanding."

About two weeks later, Buffett called Bill.

"I've been thinking about this proposition that you made me," he said. "I don't think I can let you do that. There's no upside for you. It's all downside."

"Warren, first of all, I wouldn't have it any other way," Bill said. "But second, there is some upside. The upside is that if we are successful, you are going to let us go to Las Vegas."

"Hmm," Buffett said.

CHAPTER FIFTEEN

■ ■ ■

THE BUFFETT STORE

Despite his eagerness to expand his company to Boise, Bill couldn't find time to go look at real estate. Instead, he relied on a realtor to make suggestions. After looking at demographic figures and reviewing recommended sites on an aerial map, Bill settled on a 22-acre site in Meridian, a Boise suburb. The location sounded like a prime spot for an R.C. Willey store: it was on a main street, about one half mile from the freeway. He bought the land for $2 million without even looking at it.

After the sale closed, Bill finally visited Boise to inspect the property. He was pretty disappointed. Located in a valley, the land had previously been a horse pasture. Bill had always tried to erect R.C. Willey stores on hilltops or in locations that offered great visibility. He feared that a store wouldn't stand out on this site.

"Let's look for another piece of land," he told his team. "I'll just keep this land and sell it when I can."

For the next month, representatives from R.C. Willey searched for a more suitable site. But they came up empty. The spot they had was the best one available. Itching to break ground, Bill decided to start building on the low-lying horse pasture. Before long, though, he realized he had the perfect site after all. By the summer of 1999 the building was up—a gigantic white structure with attractive blue awnings. The store was visible from every direction and was by far the most attractive building in the area. It was like having an eye-catching billboard just off the highway.

"As disappointed as I was in the beginning," Bill said, "I was elated at how attractive the building turned out."

The building was so impressive that people started showing up to shop before it was open. Bill informed Buffett that before announcing the grand opening, he planned to hold a soft opening—a preopening with little advance advertising and promotion.

For Bill, it was all about being prepared. He had learned the hard way that the last situation a retail store wants is not being ready to handle a sudden rush of customers. Bill never forgot what had happened when the R.C. Willey store ran its first newspaper advertisement in Ogden's *Standard Examiner* back in 1955. The ad was pretty generic and touted Hotpoint appliances. Nonetheless, it brought more than twenty new customers to the store within a 48-hour period. At that time, Bill was the only salesman on the floor and was used to seeing fewer than twenty customers come through his doors every week; he quickly found himself unable to attend to all the new shoppers.

As a precaution, Bill explained to Buffett that the company had adopted a method known as a "soft opening" for testing a new store's systems, from computers to warehouse delivery. Also, the sales force had an opportunity to become familiar with the merchandise, the check-out procedures, and all the important facets of customer service. In essence, a soft opening is like a dress rehearsal, ensuring that all the glitches and jitters are worked out before attracting a large opening-day crowd.

"You only get one chance to make a first impression on customers," Bill said. "If a customer has a disappointing experience on his first visit, it takes, on average, seven years to get him back."

The concept made perfect sense to Buffett. He had seen instances where huge grand-opening crowds absolutely overwhelmed the sales force, resulting in an overall bad experience for everyone—sales potentials weren't realized, employees were frustrated, and customers didn't return. A soft opening, Buffett agreed, was a wise idea.

On August 25, 1999, the Boise store opened its doors to the public for the first time. Even though it wasn't the grand opening and employees were testing and fine-tuning their systems, the store still did more than $157,000 in sales the first day. Accessories alone—such as lamps, pictures, and plaques—accounted for $17,000 in sales.

Following the first day, R.C. Willey trucks drove through the night, transporting replacement merchandise from the Salt Lake City distribution hub to Boise. When the doors opened on the second day, the store was completely restocked. At the end of the first week, Buffett called for an update. Bill reported sales had exceeded $1 million.

A few weeks later the store held its much-hyped grand opening. Buffett flew to Idaho, bringing along Irv Blumkin and other executives from the Nebraska Furniture Mart. A slew of dignitaries turned out for the ribbon cutting ceremony, led by the mayor of Boise. Before cutting the ribbon, Buffett told a story.

"When Bill wanted to build this store I was very skeptical," he told the crowd. "Then after I opened it and found out how well it was doing, I immediately had a counter-revelation and decided it was so successful that it must have been my idea. I'm really glad that Bill didn't talk me out of it."

The audience roared. For Bill, the moment couldn't have been better. "It was one of the highlights of my life," he said. "The greatest investment mind of the world was pleased with our achievement. It was a thrill to work with Warren and to see this turn into a very successful venture."

The grand opening came off without a hitch. The place was mobbed with customers, but the employees were ready and shoppers came away with an overall positive shopping experience.

While in Boise, Buffett took time out of his schedule to meet with a group of business students. Whenever R.C.

Willey had a grand opening for a new store, Buffett agreed he would speak to the business students at a university in the nearby community. At Boise State he addressed an overflow crowd of students. In his remarks, he predicted that the stock market's high-tech bubble was highly overvalued. The problem, he said, was that the high-tech stocks were trading at extraordinary high multiples, yet they had an unproven track record and very few tangible assets.

Bill had invited a friend to attend Buffett's speech. The friend was a banker whose stockbroker had been trying to persuade him to place some of his portfolio in the high-tech area. After listening to Buffett, the banker instructed his broker to cancel all scheduled high-tech stock purchases.

Eventually, the high-tech bubble did burst and Bill received a call from the banker. "I'm eternally grateful to you and Warren," he said. "That lecture saved me a little over a quarter of a million dollars."

With the Boise store flourishing, Bill and Buffett continued to talk almost daily, reviewing sales figures. When the sales figures exceeded $4 million after one month, Bill felt confident enough to sell the store to Berkshire.

"I think you ought to buy the Boise store," Bill told Buffett.

"That would be great," Buffett said. "But I'm going to pay you interest."

"No," Bill said, "we had a deal and interest wasn't included."

"Bill, we've never had an argument," Buffett said. "But we're going to have an argument over this."

Bill proposed a compromise. Buffett would pay four percent commission on sales from the last week of August through the end of November. Then Buffett would reimburse Bill for the cost of the land and the building, enabling Berkshire to take ownership of the store by December 1— just in time for the busiest shopping and delivery month of the year.

"That's not really fair to you," Buffett said. "But if that's what you want to do, that's fine."

In December, Bill received a check from Buffett for $368,000, representing the four-percent commission on sales delivered for the first three months.

In its first year, the Boise store generated $50 million in sales, nearly doubling the expectations set by Buffett. He was so impressed that he featured the success story in his annual Chairman's Letter, issued to Berkshire Hathaway shareholders at the annual meetings in Omaha. Under the heading, "A Managerial Story You Will Never Read Elsewhere," he wrote the following:

> Here's a remarkable story from last year: It's about R.C. Willey, Utah's dominant home furnishing business, which Berkshire purchased from Bill Child and his family in 1995. Bill and most of his managers are Mormons, and for this reason R.C. Willey's stores have never operated on Sunday. This is a difficult way to do business: Sunday is the favorite shopping day for many customers. Bill, nonetheless, stuck to his principles—and while

doing so built his business from $250,000 of annual sales in 1954, when he took over, to $342 million in 1999.

Bill felt that R.C. Willey could operate successfully in markets outside of Utah and in 1997 suggested that we open a store in Boise. I was highly skeptical about taking a no-Sunday policy into a new territory where we would be up against entrenched rivals open seven days a week. Nevertheless, this was Bill's business to run. So, despite my reservations, I told him to follow both his business judgment and his religious convictions.

Bill then insisted on a truly extraordinary proposition: He would personally buy the land and build the store—for about $9 million as it turned out—and would sell it to us at his cost if it proved to be successful. On the other hand, if sales fell short of his expectations, we could exit the business without paying Bill a cent. This outcome, of course, would leave him with a huge investment in an empty building. I told him that I appreciated his offer but felt that if Berkshire was going to get the upside it should also take the downside. Bill said nothing doing: If there was to be failure because of his religious beliefs, he wanted to take the blow personally.

The store opened last August and immediately became a huge success. Bill thereupon turned the property over to us—including some extra land that had appreciated significantly—and we wrote him a check for his cost. And get this: *Bill refused to take a dime of interest on the capital he had tied up over the two years.*

If a manager has behaved similarly at some other public corporation, I haven't heard about it. You can understand why the opportunity to partner with people like Bill Child causes me to tap dance to work every morning.

A footnote: After our "soft" opening in August, we had a grand opening of the Boise store about a month later. Naturally, I went there to cut the ribbon (your Chairman, I wish to emphasize, is good for *something*). In my talk I told the crowd how sales had far exceeded expectations, making us, by a considerable margin, the largest home furnishings store in Idaho. Then, as the speech progressed, my memory miraculously began to improve. By the end of my talk, it all had come back to me: Opening a store in Boise had been *my* idea.

"Bill, how come you are never satisfied?"

The question stung Bill. It came from a teary-eyed R.C. Willey salesman in 1971 after the company had experienced the most successful year in its history. Although pleased, Bill made a point to stress to the sales force that there were a number of areas that could be improved, which would enable the store to do even better the following year. That's what prompted the tough question.

The salesman's query bothered Bill for a long time,

particularly since he liked and admired the salesman so much. But ultimately Bill concluded the employee was right—Bill could never be fully satisfied. He was convinced the company could always do better. In the salesman's own mind, the sales force was doing a terrific job, and so he got upset when Bill challenged him to do better.

"You can only stand on the laurels of what you did yesterday for a few minutes," Bill said. "Then you have the challenges of tomorrow."

CHAPTER SIXTEEN

■ ■ ■

THE AMERICAN DREAM

Bill could still remember the first time the Syracuse store made $25,000 in sales in a single day. That happened in 1965. It took 27 years for the company to achieve $1 million in annual sales. But by 2000, it wasn't unusual for the company to hit $18 million in sales on a single holiday. It's easy to gloss over the years of hard work that preceded this kind of success. For example, in forty years, Bill missed only two days of work due to an illness—in 1968 when he was down with the flu. Other than that, he showed up every day unless he was taking his annual family vacation.

In order to guarantee success, the willingness to work hard must be coupled with patience. Success—real success—doesn't happen overnight. Buffett often emphasized patience, both when contemplating expansion or investing in another business. "You don't have to swing at balls," Bill heard him say on more than one occasion. "Opportunities will come."

The opportunity to open a store outside of Utah had taken decades to arrive. But now that the Boise store was flourishing, Bill figured there was no better time to ask Buffett to reconsider entering the Las Vegas market.

"Warren," Bill told him, "we've done it in Boise. Now you have to let us go to Vegas. And I'll make you the same deal as before."

"No, I can't let you do that. I can only take advantage of a guy once," Buffett said, smiling.

Bill expressed confidence that the store would succeed, even without opening on Sundays. It was difficult for Buffett to object.

"If you can do it in Vegas," Buffett said, "then you will really make a convert out of me."

In the back of his mind, Bill hoped to eventually build two R.C. Willey stores in the Las Vegas area: one in Henderson and the other in Summerlin, an exclusive 23,400-acre planned community along the western rim of the Las Vegas Valley, next door to Spring Mountains and Red Rock Canyon National Conservation Area. There was only one problem. Summerlin was controlled by The Howard Hughes Corporation, which was set up to manage the vast real estate holdings of the late Howard Hughes. The community was named after Hughes's grandmother Jean Amelia Summerlin, and no development went forward without the blessing of the corporation.

R.C. Willey made repeated overtures to the Hughes Corporation, expressing an interest in building a furniture store within the development area, but the company never even got a response. Meanwhile, Bill had already pressed forward with a store in Henderson, the company's first choice for a new location in the Las Vegas market. By 2001, the construction was complete. The soft opening was a huge success. Forty-five days later the store held its grand opening. Buffett flew out for the ribbon cutting ceremony.

With a bank of reporters looking on, Buffett cut the ribbon. As people clapped, Buffett leaned over to Bill. "Do you think we ought to announce that we're going to build another store?" Buffett whispered.

"Yes, let's do it."

Buffett then told the news media that R.C. Willey planned to build a second store in the greater Las Vegas area.

The company had not yet secured any land for a second store. But shortly after the grand opening in Henderson, Bill's office received a call from The Hughes Development Company. Unbeknownst to Bill, representatives from the development firm had visited the Henderson store. They liked what they saw and decided they wanted an R.C. Willey store in Summerlin. They called R.C. Willey's construction development manager and offered virtually any location R.C. wanted.

R.C. Willey picked some land at the end of a highway off-ramp that was still under construction. After a heavy push, the store was completed at the same time the off-ramp was ready to open for traffic.

Meanwhile, sales at the Henderson store skyrocketed, making it the most successful store in the R.C. Willey chain. Later that year, Buffett decided to use his Chairman's Letter to single out R.C. Willey again:

> Here's a postscript to a story I told you about two years ago about R.C. Willey's move to Boise. As you may remember, Bill Child, R.C. Willey's chairman, wanted to extend his home-furnishings operation beyond Utah, a state in which his company does more than $300 million of business. The company achieved this dominant position, moreover, with a "closed on Sunday" policy that defied conventional retail wisdom. I was skeptical that this policy could succeed in Boise or, for that matter, anyplace outside of Utah. After all, Sunday is the day many consumers most like to shop.
>
> As I told you in the 1999 annual report, the store immediately became a huge success—and it has since grown. . . . Shortly after the Boise opening, Bill suggested we try Las Vegas, and this time I was even more skeptical. How could we do business in a metropolis of that size and be closed on Sundays, a day that all of our competitors would be exploiting? Buoyed by the Boise experience, however, we proceeded to locate in Henderson, a mushrooming city adjacent to Las Vegas.
>
> The result: This store outsells all others in the R.C. Willey chain, doing a volume of business that far exceeds the volume of any competitor and that

is twice what I had anticipated. I cut the ribbon at that grand opening in October . . . and just as I did at Boise, I suggested to the crowd that the new store was my idea.

It didn't work. Today, when I pontificate about retailing, Berkshire people just say, "What does Bill think?" (I'm going to draw the line, however, if he suggests that we also close on Saturdays.)

The friendship between Bill and Buffett continued to grow, driven by an evolving trust that was evident early on. Months after buying R.C. Willey, Buffett invited Bill to be his dinner guest at the Alfalfa Club, an exclusive social organization that met annually in Washington, D.C. The club has been in existence since 1913 and its membership consists of the country's most influential politicians and business leaders. It is customary for the president of the United States to address the group each year. On January 27, 1996, Bill found himself seated with Buffett at a table with *Washington Post* publisher Katharine Graham, Henry Kissinger, Elliot Richardson, and Howard Baker. President Bill Clinton and Colin Powell addressed the group.

For Bill and Buffett, little things such as being honest about seemingly insignificant financial matters strengthened their relationship. For instance, after Berkshire Hathaway acquired R.C. Willey, Bill informed Buffett that his company owned a membership at one of Utah's leading country clubs. Bill felt that it was no longer appropriate for the company to carry that expense and he offered to buy the membership and take over the dues payments.

Buffett appreciated this level of integrity. One day he called Bill and extended an invitation.

"Would you like to play Augusta?" Buffett asked.

Buffett had a membership at the very exclusive Augusta National Golf Club and he planned to play golf there for a couple of days leading up to the start of that year's Master's Tournament. He explained that two of his closest friends would be joining him: Bill Gates and Tom Murphy, the legendary former CEO of Capital Cities/ABC Inc., who had recently retired following ABC's merger with Disney.

Bill was delighted. It had always been a dream of his to play the storied Master's golf course. Suddenly, he had the chance to do it with America's leading business titans.

Flattered, Bill flew to Omaha, where he joined Gates and Buffett. Together, they flew to Augusta on Buffett's private plane. Murphy met them there, and the group shared a four-room cabana not far from the clubhouse. They played golf during the day and spent the evenings talking about everything from business to world affairs to philanthropy. The conversations were fascinating. As Bill listened, questions ran through his mind.

How did a simple farm boy with aspirations of being a schoolteacher end up being a CEO?

How did a fledgling, one-room store next to a cornfield in rural Syracuse, Utah, grow into one of the nation's leading furniture chains?

And how did I end up in a room at Augusta National with

the two richest men in the world and a legendary pioneer in the television industry?

That night, Bill went to bed a firm believer in the American Dream. He had lived it, coming from hardworking parents who instilled in him bedrock character traits such as honesty, persistence, and gratitude. RC Willey's decision to launch an appliance business in a frontier town was the perfect backdrop to Bill's sense of pride and trust in a family-owned operation. Bill never set out to be a millionaire or impress a guy like Warren Buffett, but that's precisely what impressed Buffett. R.C. Willey Home Furnishings was a throwback to another time in America. Yet the company had proved its ability to adapt and reach the top in the twenty-first century.

On the last day at Augusta, Bill ducked into a restroom at the clubhouse before his foursome started the back nine. He overheard a group of men who were playing cards in the clubhouse. "We've got quite a foursome out here today," one of them said to the others. "We've got Bill Gates, Warren Buffett, Tom Murphy, and some other guy."

Bill took it as a great compliment to be referred to as the "other guy" in the group.

BILL CHILD

■ ■ ■

AFTERWORD

Selling R.C. Willey Home Furnishings to Warren Buffett was the climax of my business career. Warren got a great company and I solved two problems: inheritance and guaranteeing that the business would continue beyond my lifetime. It was a win-win situation for both parties. Plus, I got the added bonus of working with Warren, a man I admire and respect for his honesty, his values, and his integrity, not to mention the blessing of having access to a man with one of the most brilliant business minds of our time.

My business journey is proof that the American Dream is still alive and well. In recent years many have suggested that I write a book about my experiences and our company's unlikely path to success. I have always felt strongly that the R.C. Willey story should be told. But when Warren also encouraged the idea, I decided to act. Since I am not a writer, I commissioned author Jeff Benedict to tell our story. Although I have supplemented most of the expense to have the book written, I will receive none of the profits. All profits will go to the author and the publisher. If the book does very well, surplus profits will be donated to charities.

Personally, I'm not interested in royalties or publicity. My motivation is simply to share our story with the countless thousands of associates, business partners, and customers who have been such a big part of R.C. Willey's success. I hope lessons learned from these pages will benefit anyone interested in achieving success, from seasoned executives to aspiring business students to individuals trying to organize their personal finances.

In life there are many "what-if" moments. Looking back I realize that on more than one occasion our company's future hinged on a single decision. Here are just a few examples:

What if I had taken the banker's advice and sold or closed the store shortly after RC turned it over to me in 1954? The banker saw me as an inexperienced kid taking over a retail business that I knew nothing about. But I saw a business with a great reputation and a loyal customer base. Closing the business would not have been in anyone's best interest. Had I listened to the experts and taken the easy way out, my business career would have been over before it started.

What if I had not decided to add furniture to our inventory? We would have remained a small appliance store in rural Syracuse, Utah, no doubt closing our doors when bigger box stores came on the scene.

What if my brother Sheldon had not decided to join me, choosing instead to teach school? I would not have had his counsel and expertise for the next thirty-four years.

What if we had not decided to expand and build a second store in Murray?

What if we had not decided to use television advertising when our competitors were ignoring it? We wouldn't have had the huge growth that our company experienced.

What if we had been too afraid to offer direct financing to our customers? We would have missed the opportunity of setting up our successful credit operation.

What if we had not reinvested our profits into our infrastructure by building a central distribution center?

What if I had selfishly sold the company to one of the investment banks that offered us more than $200 million?

What if I had not inquired as to whether Warren might have an interest in buying our company?

What if I had not made Warren a deal he could not turn down in order to build the Boise store? We would not have expanded out of state and we would not now have stores in Boise, Reno, Las Vegas, and Sacramento. Today we are doing more business outside of the state of Utah than inside.

What if Rufus Call Willey had not been forced by his competitors to build a 600 square-foot appliance store next to his house in 1948? Probably none of the above would have happened. The company no doubt would have died, and RC would have been remembered simply as a great door-to-door salesman.

It is easy to see how a single decision or the unwillingness to change can sink a company. At one time or another we had more than forty-five competitors in Utah. Only one or two of them remain in business. That fact has prompted many people, in and out of the furniture business, to ask me how we were able to be so successful when so many others failed. A lot of our success boils down to steady adherence to some simple management principles and philosophies that guided my forty-eight-year-career as CEO of R.C. Willey.

1. Be motivated by excellence, not money. You need to be better than all of your competitors. If you are, the profits will come.

2. Offer customers true value on quality products. A low price on a cheap piece of furniture is not value.

3. Think like a customer and treat them as you would like to be treated. Remember: we are agents for our customers and they can fire us at any time and take their business elsewhere.

4. Enjoy your business and know the industry and its future.

5. Avoid unnecessary debt. When the economy takes a downturn, excessive debt will sink you.

6. Be efficient. Nothing drains profits like waste.

7. Treat your associates with respect; otherwise employees won't treat customers with respect.

8. Pay attention to details. To borrow a phrase from Warren—In retail, you need to be good every day.

9. Be honest! Nothing sinks a reputation faster than dishonesty. It takes years to build a reputation, but it can be destroyed in one day over one misdeed.

10. Hire good and capable people—people you respect and will enjoy working with.

11. Make decisions with an eye to the future, not just what is good for today.

12. Differentiate your company with marketing; don't always follow the crowd. At times you must go outside the box. Good marketing creates immediate sales and top-of-mind awareness for your product and your company.

13. Most important, be able to adapt to changes in the marketplace and don't be afraid to change when circumstances demand. We live in a changing world.

There is one other lesson I have learned over the years and that is the importance of saying thank you. The significance of those two words is easily overlooked in business. A leader can't get far without good people behind him. I have had the privilege of working beside thousands of exceptional associates over a long career—too many to mention. Hopefully they know how much I truly appreciate them.

Likewise, outside the company I have many terrific business associates, too many to single out here. But I am particularly indebted to the Blumkin family, especially Irv for introducing the R.C. Willey family to the Berkshire Hathaway family.

Running a business can put an awful strain upon a family. Without my lovely wife, Pat, I am sure my company and my family wouldn't be where they are today. For more than forty years, Pat displayed patience and support far more impressive than anything that shows up on a balance sheet. I am also grateful to our eight children, all of whom have worked in the business, helping it to grow; in particular, our son Steve, who has spent more than thirty years managing and growing the appliance and electronic departments of our business. My daughter Tammy, son Mike, and sons-in-law, John Peterson and Troy Markham, have all made big contributions. My personal secretaries over the years have become family. I don't know what I would have done without Marcia Garner and Sherry Gross. I can't say enough about my brother, Sheldon. He wasn't just my partner for forty years; he was a trusted, loyal friend.

I always felt that Sheldon would eventually run the business. But when his circumstances changed, his son-in-law, Scott Hymas, along with Sheldon's two sons, Jeff and Curtis Child, took over the business. All three had been working for our company for a number of years and they easily transitioned into their executive roles.

I would also like to pay tribute to my parents, who stood by my side through thick and thin. Dad taught me how to work and the value and importance of honesty, as well as the benefit of having and protecting a good name. Mother taught me love and patience, and I treasure her undying support for her family.

Above all, I probably owe much of my professional success to two men: Rufus Call Willey and Warren Buffett. RC introduced me to the world of retail business. He was a mentor, who taught me by example. If a customer said he needed more time to think about an appliance purchase, RC would say, "Why don't you just take this $5 and go have lunch on me while you're thinking about it. And whatever you decide will be okay." The couple would go out to the car, talk it over, and more often than not, a few minutes later they would return and make the purchase. He knew how to understand and handle people. He never twisted anyone's arm or used high-pressure sales tactics. He always did what he thought was best for the customer.

As much as I learned from him about sales and business, RC taught me even more about life. He loved the outdoors and would often take me hunting, but he'd never shoot anything. "Bill, let me tell you something," he once said when we were tracking deer. "We can have a wonderful time until you shoot one of those animals. That's when the fun stops and the work begins." He had a wonderful zest for living life to its fullest and he realized that there were other priorities in life besides work and business.

What a blessing to have had him as a mentor and a

father-in-law. I am grateful for his love and support, as well as his lovely daughter Darline. She gave me four children and fourteen wonderful years of marriage. My commitment to her and RC had a lot to do with my decision to hold on to the business.

Warren's influence came at the end of my career. Irv Blumkin said, "Warren Buffett is the perfect partner." I could not agree more. He's been a wonderful mentor, teacher, and example of sharing and giving back of one's time and talents. He has always been available to answer a phone call, give insight on a question, and help me come to a conclusion that I think is my own. His management style should be taught in all business classes across the nation. He trusts and supports management, and he lets them make their own decisions as long as they are honest and forthright in their stewardship. He only wants to control capital expenditures. He has shared his wisdom and knowledge with thousands of university students.

I remember one particular experience when I helped bring approximately forty students from the University of Utah and Brigham Young University to Omaha. We flew out of Salt Lake City in a heavy snowstorm that dumped approximately eighteen inches and delayed our arrival into Omaha, where even more snow had fallen. The entire city had been shut down. We arrived late to Warren's office, but he spoke to the students and answered their questions for more than ninety minutes and then left to have a root canal, saying if he felt well enough he would possibly rejoin us. He called a restaurant asking them to stay open because the restaurant where we had reservations had already closed due to the weather. After we were seated, Warren came back from the dentist and spent another two hours, moving from table to table, talking to the students, and answering any questions. He also picked up the tab for our dinner. On the flight back, the students were still in awe. It was a life-changing experience. Many said that it was a pivotal day in their college careers.

Because Warren has spoken to overflowing crowds at the universities in the cities where we have had store grand openings, I still have students comment on his visit to BYU more than twelve years ago. When I have spoken to students and business people, I have told them that if they ever have a chance to associate with or be a partner with Warren Buffett, to do it and do it fast. It will be the best decision of your life. So thank you, Warren, for your tremendous influence on so many lives, particularly young business students.

BILL CHILD

Author's Note

In 2003, Bill Child retired as CEO of R.C. Willey Home Furnishings and assumed the position of chairman of the board of directors. He and his wife, Pat, went on to serve a two-year service mission for The Church of Jesus Christ of Latter-day Saints, overseeing the Visitors' Center at the Washington D.C. Temple. Bill's relationship with Warren Buffett has continued to grow.

The R.C. Willey business continues to be a jewel in the Berkshire Hathaway portfolio. In 2006, the company opened a store in Sacramento, California, bringing the total number of stores in the chain to eleven. In 2007, the company's value topped the $1 billion mark.

INDEX

165

INDEX